Stalking
the
Faraway Places

Other books by Euell Gibbons:

Stalking the Wild Asparagus
Stalking the Healthful Herbs
Stalking the Good Life
Stalking the Blue-eyed Scallop
Beachcomber's Handbook
Feast on a Diabetic Diet
  (*with Joe Gibbons*)

Stalking the Faraway Places

by EUELL GIBBONS

illustrated by
FREDA GIBBONS

David McKay Company, Inc.
New York

STALKING THE FARAWAY PLACES

COPYRIGHT © 1973 BY EUELL GIBBONS

Portions of this book have appeared, in slightly
different form, in *Frontiers Magazine*,
Boys' Life Magazine, *Organic Gardening and Farming Magazine*,
Natural History Magazine and *Natural Geographic Magazine*.

LIBRARY OF CONGRESS CATALOG CARD NUMBER: 73–79955
ISBN: 0–679–50394–3
MANUFACTURED IN THE UNITED STATES OF AMERICA

Contents

v

III. Botanical Wonders

IV. The Whimsical Side of Mother Nature

I look around me, see our land with junk-cars piled on every hand—billboards obstructing every view—a parking lot where trees once grew—polluted air—polluted streams—eroded soil and broken dreams—a rising crime rate—crowded jails.

Are humans really smart as snails?

—From "The Snail" * by Euell Gibbons

* Originally published in *Frontiers,* a publication of the Academy of Natural Sciences of Philadelphia.

I. Exploring

the

Faraway Places

1. Stalking the Daydream

I'VE BEEN daydreaming again. Forty-five years ago I lived on a homestead in the Navajo Indian country of northwestern New Mexico, a fairly high altitude region with severe winters. How we welcomed spring—and not least because it meant a change of diet! Those who have grown up in these days of supermarkets and frozen foods may have trouble understanding how we craved fresh, green vegetables.

The first green edibles were never domesticated plants, for nature offers wild greens at least a month before it is time to even plant the garden. We fairly gobbled salads made of peppergrass, wild mustards, and dandelions. Plants we would fight as weeds later were welcome now. Russian thistle, just peeping through the ground, was gathered and cooked like spinach, and after a winter of vitamin-deficient meals these greens tasted like ambrosia. No wonder I grew up with a taste for wild foods!

My knowledge of edible wild plants has vastly increased since those days. My joy in remembering them is alloyed

3

with regret when I think of all the delicious wild foods that we could have used to add interest, variety, and healthful nutrition to our rather meager, monotonous spring diet. I find myself nostalgically sighing that old man's cliché, "I wish I could do it all over again with the knowledge that I have now."

Well, why not? What's to prevent me going out there this spring and enjoying all the wild foods I missed when I was a boy?

The daydream takes over. My wife, Freda, and I will drive out in our camper, and pick up our two eldest grandchildren, Mike, thirteen, and Colleen, eleven, who live in Albuquerque. They're wild about wild food and both of them are good campers and hikers. We'll take along back-packing gear so we can leave the camper and penetrate roadless areas at will. Not only will we pick and enjoy the overlooked foods, we'll live on them for a week or two, carrying only a few civilized seasonings to make them palatable to our overcivilized tastes.

Were you ever faced with a dream come true? It can be a disconcerting experience. Moving from fantasy to fact means moving from perfect to imperfect. A ten-mile hike carrying a thirty-pound pack, when made in a daydream, leaves me fresh as a daisy. But when it's made over rocky hills it will leave me bone weary. The daydreams were of finding, cooking, and eating great quantities of wild foods. They included very little of the often fruitless, disappointing search that reality will demand. In dreams, nature showers me with seductive, euphonious plants such as sweet cicely, roseroot, passionfruit, and virgin's bower; but in reality she is likely to offer me naked broomrape and bastard toadflax.

Yet for better or worse we are going, despite the certain hard work, the possible hunger and hardships. We shall go to the only spot in the United States where four states corner—New Mexico, Arizona, Utah, and Colorado—and work out from there. We shall be surrounded by Indians, the vast Navajo reservation occupying adjacent New Mexico, Arizona, and Utah, and the Southern Utes in southwestern Colorado. These are my brothers, the companions of my boyhood, and I feel perfectly confident that my abundantly haired scalp will remain intact.

What will we find to eat in this barren land? In the first place it isn't all that barren. The San Juan River flows here, and in its valley are woods and marshes. Lofty, snow-covered mountains loom above the valleys, and around the mesas that make the foothills there are nut pine, juniper, and ponderosa pine forests. There are grasslands and sagebrush flats. True, there is real desert nearby, but in early spring it blossoms into a vast flowerbed, and some of the desert plants are edible.

We'll find a marsh with tules growing in the shallows. These bulrushes (*Scirpus acutus* and closely allied species) show tender sprouts in April. Peeled to the white heart, they are crisp, mild, and sweet, a far better vegetable than celery hearts or the white interior of head lettuce. The perennial rhizomes from which they spring are up to 1½ inches in diameter, and you can often get sections two to three feet long by simply pulling them out of the mud. When these scaly ropes are peeled they show a core of rich, starchy food with some fibers. The outer end, with its new bud, isn't even fibrous. These taste better cooked. They are about twelve percent carbohydrate and one percent protein, with the rest pure marshwater. There is no shortage of tules—and no one need go hungry when they grow.

We'll also find agave or century plant (*Agave utahensis*) on the desert hills. For years each plant has stored starch and sugar in its mighty heart, and this becomes not only edible but actually delicious when cooked slowly in an underground oven. The budding flower stalk, when it is just starting, is a fine vegetable, as are the flower stalks of the yucca, another abundant desert plant.

There will be a profusion of nopalitos, the new-grown flattened stem joints of the prickly pear cactus (*Opuntia* species). With the sticker clusters removed and cut into green bean-sized slices, this is a very wholesome and palatable vegetable, rich in vitamins A and C, as well as containing considerable carbohydrate and protein.

What about animal proteins and fats? We may catch a few carp or catfish from the San Juan. We might even enjoy some pork—or maybe I should spell it porc—from the porcupines that abound in the piñon and pine woods around the mesas. They are easily procured. We might even snare some cottontails or prairie dogs for meat. The prairie dog is edible, being a rodent akin to our eastern squirrels and having similar meat. But we won't worry too much if these animals don't find their way into our cooking pots. We will all be carrying a few extra pounds around the waistline that can make up any deficiencies for a few days. I could easily donate ten pounds to this worthy cause if it came off the right places!

Protein and fat are essential in the diet over the long haul, but I have found that on survival trips one should first seek out a dependable and abundant supply of carbohydrates. These are quickly digested and furnish fuel to keep the brain operating. Let your brain get underfed and then all interest, enthusiasm, and spirit to go on with the experience tend to melt. First get starch fed, then add the trimmings. When eating fresh wild food plants the same day they are picked, it becomes impossible to develop a vitamin shortage.

Along the valley I hope to find old friends, like lamb's-quarters (*Chenopodium album*), rough pigweed (*Amaranthus* species), wild lettuce (*Lactuca scariola*), and any number of other potherbs that will make a tasty salad dish.

Then there are the wintered-over roots of wild and delicious cousins of the domestic carrot, the biscuitroot (*Cymopterus bulbosas*), the Indian potato (*Orogenia linearifolia*), and the yampa or wild caraway (*Perideridia gairdneri*). These are sweeter, even a little larger, in the spring than they are in the fall.

While that area will not furnish the great plenty that I find in such fruitful places as Pennsylvania and Maine, I know it will feed us. We can't be as choosy about our food as we could in most places where I forage; we will probably have to treasure everything that is even remotely edible—but we'll have fun and come out in good shape.

Does it take courage to plunge into such an adventure? Not at all. We are not risking our lives, only our comfort. We expect—we even hope—that we won't find it too easy. Nature often hands out a few hardships along with her other bounty.

2. Wild Foods
of the West

MY WIFE, two grandchildren, and I drove out of Shiprock, New Mexico, early in the morning searching for edible wild plants. Mike, our thirteen-year-old grandson, was sitting next to me in the front seat of our camper. Suddenly he pointed toward some green plants with bright purple blooms making a spot of color in this otherwise drab landscape. "Grandpa, what are those pretty plants?" he asked. I told him this was the famous locoweed and explained how horses sometimes ate it, indeed developed a craving for it, even though continued eating of locoweed will drive a horse insane. Mike said, "Let's stop and eat some of it, then maybe we'll be crazy enough to go ahead with the trip."

The local people, even the Indians, considered us daft when we told them we were trying to find enough wild foods to live on in this arid, barren, overgrazed, high-altitude land in the middle of April. I had been a teenager in this same country back in the 1920s and had ranged the length and breadth of this big land on horseback. Then one could find places where a horse could eat his fill in the circle covered by a thirty-foot lariat rope tied to a stake. I could find enough wild food to stave off starvation for a week at the time, and I knew far less about wild food then than I know now.

But the country has deteriorated. Rainfall has decreased and overgrazing has increased. We encouraged the Indians to build costly houses rather than cost-free hogans. We encouraged them to drive expensive pickups that eat high-priced gasoline, rather than horses that raised themselves on the open range, fueled with grass. We gave these noble Red Men a taste of processed food, store-bought clothes, hamburgers, and whiskey. It needs cash, in considerable quantities to support such a life, so each Indian family increased its herds and they vied with one another for the scanty grass this land produces. The land retaliated by producing even less. I was able to locate a few of the identical spots where I tethered my horse to eat his fill forty-five years ago, only to find them bare and gullied now.

Blaming the paucity of food plants on Navajo sheep, we drove into the Ute country of southwestern Colorado, only to find the Ute cattle can eat as many of the precious edible wild plants as can sheep. The Utes were once a food-gathering tribe. When we questioned some Ute women about wild food plants we found that they had forgotten the plants that fed their ancestors, but they showed us a place where we could gather wild asparagus, an introduced plant that has recently gone wild there. Ever since I wrote the book *Stalking the Wild Asparagus*, this plant seems to pursue me. However, we were getting a bit desperate, so we filled a bag with fat asparagus spears.

We drove north out of the Indian country and found that white men's cattle were overgrazing the land as badly as the Indian-owned livestock. The road map showed a back way down an intermittent stream in Utah. Things began to look up. At a bend in the wash we found a patch of green and stopped. There we gathered a great quantity of sea blite, *Suaeda depressa*, an old friend we had often eaten on the islands of Maine. There it grows by the seaside and is heavily impregnated with salt. Here it is called "seepweed" and it grows in damp spots of saline soil and tastes almost as salty as it does in Maine. It is a palatable vegetable, whether raw or cooked.

Here we also found young tumbleweed, *Salsola kali*, only a few inches high. It is also called Russian thistle, and when old it is covered with hard stickers. It forms great balls that break loose from their roots when the seed is ripe. The balls roll across the plains when strong winds blow, scattering their seeds everywhere. Most Westerners consider it a pestiferous weed and don't realize that the young plants, before the stickers harden, make a succulent, palatable vegetable when cooked like spinach. Indeed, this plant is a close relative of spinach, as is the salty seepweed. Colleen, my eleven-year-old granddaughter, and Mike pinched these tender plants so enthusiastically that we soon had enough to feed twice our number.

We also found, in great abundance, tumble mustard, *Sisymbrium altissimum*, and tansy mustard, *Descurainia Sophia*, but these were both blooming. They are supposed to make good potherbs only when young and tender. Since they were so eminently available we gathered a supply of each anyway, trying to take only the tenderest and most recently grown parts of each plant. We saw, but did not gather, povertyweed, *Monolepis nuttalliana*, and peppergrass, or poor man's pepper, *Lepidium campestre*. Maybe the common names put us off, but how many kinds of "greens" can you eat at one setting?

Even the dry hills yielded some goodies. A narrow-leaved yucca, *Yucca standleyi*, was just showing its asparaguslike bloomstalk above the sharp-pointed leaves. We found and

tumble mustard

(Sisymbrium altissimum)

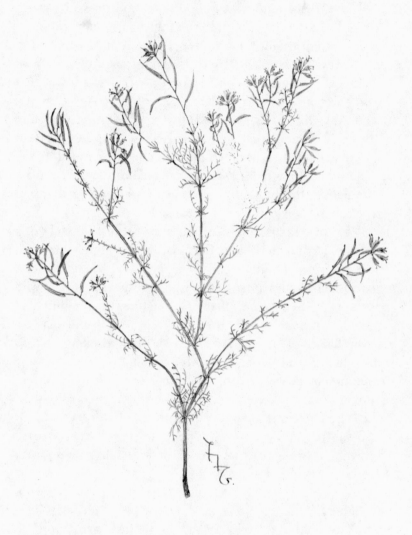

tansy mustard

(*Descurainia Sophia*)

garnered several dozen. Then there was the strange joint-fir, *Ephedra Torreyana*, which appears to be leafless; its leaves are reduced to tiny scales at the joints. The bare twigs are yellowish green and the life processes that are conducted in the leaves of most plants are relegated to the surface layers of these bare branches, a water-conserving arrangement that works well in this arid climate. Two of the many common names by which this plant is called are "Mormon tea" and "Brigham Young tea." It is an excellent camp beverage for our first wild dinner in Utah. Drinking this desert tea is supposed to confer all kinds of medical benefits, from stimulating the appetite to curing syphilis. We drank it regularly on this trip merely because we liked it.

We pitched our camp near the ruined stone buildings of a pre-pueblo Indian village that had stood untenanted for about seven hundred years. I doubt that these ancient, semi-agricultural people ever prepared a meal as totally wild as the one we cooked on that site. We found that nature had provided greater variety than a camp cook could conveniently handle. One can carry only so many cooking utensils into the wild and there is a limited amount of room over any campfire small enough to be approached. We could either cook a number of kinds together or we could cook and eat the different kinds serially. We chose the latter method, for we wanted to become familiar with the flavor of each individual species before we started blending them into esoteric concoctions.

We were six people, including David Hiser, the National Geographic photographer, and his helper, Terri McGraw, who had enthusiastically joined us in tasting nature. We made Mormon tea by adding a large handful of recently cut Ephedra stems to a six-quart pot of water, boiling it a few minutes, then allowing it to steep until cool enough to drink. All pronounced the flavor and aroma satisfactory, nothing to go into ecstacies about, but a good, every day sort of drink with a taste that promised to wear well. The naturally salted seepweed proved to be oversalted when boiled. We solved this by draining off the salty potlikker and using it for water in which to cook the young tumbleweed. Thus processed they both were turned into tender, palatable vegetables well liked by the whole party. Colleen took a bite of every vegetable, a sip of Mormon tea, and announced, "I could make a whole meal on food like this." Mike reminded her, "That's exactly what you'll have to do if you don't want to go to bed hungry."

Next we tried the tumble mustard and the tansy mustard. Boiled and salted we found them bitter, aromatic, and awful. We forced down only a few bites. I said the records were plain that the Indians had used tansy mustard as a food plant and suggested this might be an acquired taste. Colleen told me she didn't expect to live long enough to learn to like tansy mustard. As Freda poured soap flakes into the dishwater some blew into the tansy mustard pot and Mike took another taste and announced, "That's the first time I ever tasted a flavor that could be improved by adding soap." We ate some more seepweed and tumbleweed, filled up on Mormon tea, and went to bed. I expected hunger pangs during the night. Greens must be nourishing, for all slept well.

At breakfast we boiled the yucca bloomstalks and found them quite bitter. Only the youngest bloom buds tasted edible to our spoiled palates. There is a good flavor beyond the bitterness, but we had trouble getting to it. I quartered the wild asparagus spears and fried them in cooking oil to give us some much-needed fat. This was a popular food; and with leftover seepweed and tumbleweed, and many cups of hot Mormon tea, we made a good breakfast.

We drove into the Utah desert between Blanding and Lake Powell. The desert wildflowers were beautiful, and among them were the white, four-petaled flowers of the spectacle plant, *Dithyrea wislizenii.* The flat twin seedpods look like tiny sunglasses. Leaves, tender stems, flowers, buds, and green seedpods all tasted good, hinting of garlic and horseradish. Mike developed the technique of stripping the stalks with a soft grip that removed only the tender parts. We gathered a bagful. After pitching camp at Irish Green Springs (which must have been named by a land developer), we had a tasting bee to decide how spectacle plant should be cooked. Behind the good flavor was a little astringency that I suspected was tannin, a substance often abounding in desert plants. I reasoned that, if milk in tea will tame down the tannin and make strong tea taste mild, then the same thing should work with spectacle plant. We boiled it, adding some powdered milk to the cooking water. While it was boiling Mike sniffed the air and said, "That smells exactly like pepperoni pizza." This promised well, and the dish was good.

All about our camp the prickly pear, some sort of *Opuntia,* flourished. Of course there was no fruit in April, the flower buds were just starting to develop, but the flattened joints, usually called "leaves" by the unbotanical, were tender and fleshy. We gathered a supply and started experimenting on ways to get the edible, inside flesh out of its spiny exterior. Burning them off in the campfire didn't work too well for us, for it left the tiny, hairlike bristles, called "glochids," to deal misery to fingers, lips, and tongue. I learnedly explained that these tiny spines could cause discomfort but were probably not dangerous, as they had been detected in ninety percent of the feces examined in the exploration of the Mesa Verde Indian Ruins. Mike unkindly pointed out that the Mesa Verde Indians were all dead.

I finally developed a satisfactory technique for removing the skin of the cactus pods with its spines and bristles. While holding a pad down on a board I sliced the spiny edges away with a fish-fillet knife, then sliced off the top and bottom

skins leaving the stickerless, juicy tender interior. Raw they
were mucilaginous, but had no bad flavor; in fact they had
little flavor of any kind. Boiled they left a slimy, ropy juice.
Those of us who appreciated boiled okra found them
tolerable, but nothing special. I cut some of the filleted pads
in slender strips, rolled them in flour, and fried them in
cooking oil. This was easily the best way to prepare this
vegetable, and the flour and oil furnished us with badly
needed fats and carbohydrates. This and Mormon tea was
our supper and immediately after eating we spread our
sleeping bags under the stars and were soon dreaming.

Next morning we indulged ourselves in pancakes and sugar
syrup, for our energy was beginning to lag on the meager wild
food we had found so far in this desert. We set off to explore,
up a dry wash, and soon came on great numbers of thistles
growing at the bottom of the arroyo (*Cirsium*, species not
determined). There are no poisonous thistles and many have
edible roots, crowns, and flower stalks. The roots of these
were disappointing, but the crowns and flower stalks seemed
good so we gathered a great quantity. Then Freda insisted
that the oversized dock (*Rumex hymenosepalus*) that was
growing in great abundance on the dry hills could be used as
domestic rhubarb. Raw it tasted almost exactly like rhubarb.
We gathered a great quantity of the stout leaf stems.

Our topographical map showed a cliff-dweller's ruin to one
side of the wash, and when we came to it we were amazed at
its state of preservation. Many of the tiny rooms were intact,
even to the juniper timbers the Indians used for ceilings. It
had not been vandalized, and broken pottery and very tiny
corncobs were all about. I warned the children that we must
take nothing but pictures and leave nothing but footprints.
Here was a wonderful record of some of our country's
prehistoric dwellers and we must do nothing to deface it.
One open place under the overhanging cliff apparently
served as the social center and grist mill of this little Indian

dock

(*Rumex hymenosepalus*)

settlement. Several *metates*, or grinding places, had been worn in the living rock that made up the floor, depressions worn smooth by thousands of rubs with the hand grinding stones the people used to grind their cultivated corn and wild seeds. We sat in the same place and prepared our thistle crowns, peeled thistle-bloom stalks, and peeled stems of the dock that we had gathered, feeling a close kinship with the ancient peoples who once lived here.

I found the immediate neighborhood of these ruins very interesting, botanically. The rhubarb dock, Mormon tea, prickly pear, and the thistle we had been gathering grew more plentifully near the ruins than elsewhere. Just below the ruins was almost a thicket of serviceberry in full bloom. Within two months these would be loaded with purplish-black berries that are very sweet and wholesome. Growing almost under the overhanging cliff was the sacred datura, a drug plant used by some Indian tribes to induce visions, by which they were guided. Did these semi-agricultural primitives have anything to do with the fact that these plants grew here? We found serviceberry and sacred datura nowhere else in this area.

We tried to take a shortcut back across the mesa to camp, but found it a very tiring longcut instead. We cooked the dock leaf stems with sugar and found them indistinguishable in taste from domestic rhubarb. The thistles were excellent boiled and seasoned; and so, with Mormon tea, we made a good meal.

The next day we decided to try to cook some of this native produce in an underground oven, without utensils. Mike wanted to make the oven. I told him to dig an oblong hole a couple of feet deep, line the bottom and sides with stones, build a fire in it, and then put more stones in the fire to heat, while the rest of us gathered the food. Mike worked so conscientiously that his carefully lined oven soon resembled

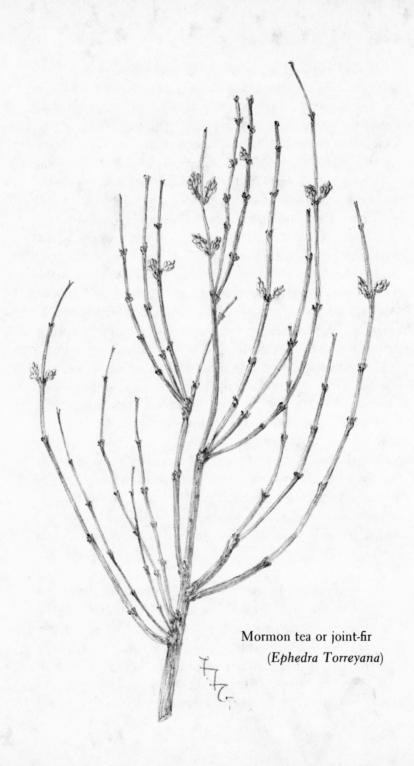

Mormon tea or joint-fir
(*Ephedra Torreyana*)

a well-laid flagstone patio. He kept the fire going until the stones were almost white-hot.

Our reference books said that tansy mustard was more palatable steamed than boiled. We therefore made up a cheesecloth bag of it. Other bags contained spectacle plant, peeled and sliced prickly pear pads, and some of the leaves of the rhubarb dock, which were recommended in our sources as good greens. We also gathered a great pile of tumble mustard, which was the most abundant plant in the area, not to eat, but to use as a steaming agent in the underground oven. We wet this weed with water from the spring, raked out the fire, covered the hot rocks with weed, then put in our food bags, covered them with more wet weed, put on the loose hot rocks, added another layer of wet tumble mustard, and finally covered everything with a layer of soil to hold in the steam.

When we opened it, it smelled good. This is an excellent way to cook good food, but I'm afraid ours wasn't that good. Even this cooking method won't turn bad-tasting things into delicacies. The tansy mustard probably would have been nourishing but the flavor was still impossible to our palates. It might be edible when very young, but the samples we tried didn't promise much. The dock leaves were very acid, as though they had been drenched in vinegar, but they were edible, and even palatable in small quantities. The spectacle plant had been much better when cooked with milk. This steamed vegetable was bitter and somewhat astringent. I tried mixing the vegetables together and that improved them a little, but they still weren't good. The cactus pads had been much better fried; these steamed ones didn't have a bad flavor but the slimy, mucilaginous texture put most of the party off. We rekindled the fire, made some dough of biscuit mix, patted it into thin cakes, and made Navajo fried bread. This, with leftover sweet-dock sauce and Mormon tea, was eagerly eaten. Our conclusions were that the desert could furnish food that would hold body and soul together at this time of year, but it produces very little that even a wild food freak would call delicious.

Our next project was really wild. We planned to pick an area from the map where I had never been before, don our backpacks, walk into it, and stay for three days, carrying no food whatever. As usual, David Hiser and I argued about the location of this adventure. David wanted it to be on the verge of some high mesa where he could photograph the entire West at one exposure, while I wanted it in some more or less fertile canyon where wild food grew. My arguments proved to be better campaign material, so the rest of the group voted with me. We chose a roadless area of the lower Dolores Canyon at its confluence with the Colorado River.

It was touching, and a bit frightening, to see the faith the crew had in my ability to find enough wild food to feed us. They not only willingly walked away from the locked camper, but they were in a holiday mood. I must confess to a bit of anxiety. I had a vision of an uncomfortable wife and two suffering grandchildren sitting around an empty campfire condemning me with hungry looks. My foraging eye was never sharper than on that hike into our wilderness campsite.

We soon saw plenty of prickly pear pads, the kind we had been eating, and Mormon tea was abundant. Those peeled prickly pear pads were going to be hard to take with no flour to bread them, no oil to fry them, and no salt to season them, but they might hold body and soul together boiled in river water and washed down with Mormon tea. When the trail reached the flats near the Dolores River I began to breathe easier. Saltbush (*Atriplex canescens*) bordered the trail, loaded with newly grown tender leaves and shoots. This was a ready-salted vegetable so palatable we enjoyed eating it raw as we walked along. Under the bushes grew a low, mealy lamb's-quarters in great abundance and two species of peppergrass, *Lepidium*, dotted the ground. Our old friends scepweed and tumbleweed also showed here and there, promising that we need not go hungry nor suffer a vitamin shortage.

Mike quartered the range ahead of us like a good bird dog, and I heard him call from up a little side canyon. By the time I arrived he was digging wild onions with his hands and already had a good bunch of them. Patches of onion flowers, *Allium geyeri*, made intermittent white-and-pink carpets all around. We were so overjoyed at this discovery that we filled a great bag with onions. If one must live on vegetable stews, onions for flavor can be a blessing.

As we gathered onion, I explained that biscuitroot (*Cymopterus* species) should be found in this area and in exactly this kind of habitat. I described the plant, and Freda looked down and said, "I think you are standing on one." Sure enough, the white flower and lacy foliage of one of these low, inconspicuous plants were protruding from beneath the sole of my shoe. We all looked at it long enough to train our eyes to see it, then we spread out and found it in unlimited abundance.

Laden with food, we found a sheltered place to camp. Shelter is needed here, for a very strong wind often blows up the Colorado. We went to the river and found an eddy. We had lines and hooks and we had stopped by the roadside and picked up a discarded Coke bottle. I had learned Coke-bottle fishing in Mexico, so showed Mike how to wind his monofilament line around the narrow place in the bottle and put his sinker and hook on the free end. Bait was a real problem. After much digging we found two white grubs. One swings the baited end of line around one's head then throws it outward, pointing the base of the bottle outward at the same time. The line peels off the bottle like it does from a spinning reel. To retrieve it, one turns the bottle crosswise and winds in the line.

nodding wild onion

(*Allium cernuum*)

Mike quickly mastered this method of casting, and he soon landed a small catfish. He cut it open and pointed out that its red entrails resembled earthworms. He threaded one of these on his hook and soon pulled in a decent sized carp. We saw that we had an ever-replenishing source of bait, that the fish were biting hungrily, and that we were not likely to go hungry. We were very happy.

Freda prepared a pot of fish, a pot of mixed saltbush, onion, and peppergrass, a pot of biscuitroot, and a pot of Mormon tea. A very satisfying meal. The saltbush salted the whole thing adequately. The mixed vegetable dish was especially good. The biscuitroot was a mixed bag of young roots, older, tougher ones, and very old ones that were almost pure fiber. The flavor was good, slightly reminiscent of carrots and parsnips, and the young, tender ones were very fine, an excellent survival food often found in areas where other foods are likely to be very scarce.

Next morning Freda added lamb's-quarters, wild onions, seepweed, saltbush, and biscuitroot tops to the fish broth, and it made a good dish though not a very breakfasty one. Then we gathered biscuitroot, more carefully this time, taking only the young, tender ones. We renewed our supply of wild onions. Then we found fishhook cactus, a small barrel cactus less than a foot high. I cleaned it as I would a pineapple and the resulting rings even tasted a bit like pineapple, if I exercised my imagination enough. Eaten raw it made a very good salad. Mike had continued his success at Coke-bottle fishing and had eight catfish. We broiled them over coals, as a change from having everything boiled. With biscuitroot, broiled fish, cactus salad, and the inevitable Mormon tea, we made a good meal and went to bed satisfied.

The next day we decided to try for a feast on all the edibles we discovered. We first breakfasted on fish boiled in a strong saltbush broth, a good technique, as fish need salt to be good. Then we ranged the bottomlands and the hills gathering food. We found some young tumbleweed, lots of peppergrass, and we cleaned great bags of wild onions. Saltbush shoots, lamb's-quarters, seepweed, and biscuitroot exhausted our vegetable possibilities. Mike came running from the fishing hole shouting that he caught a catfish three feet long. We decided on a wilderness bouillabaisse with a cactus salad for our big meal. We boiled the vegetables, then added boneless catfish fillets. It was adequately salted with saltbush, and, while it didn't taste much like a French bouillabaisse, it was a wonderful survivors' stew; and, with boiled biscuitroot, fishhook cactus rings, and Mormon tea we felt that we had dined well.

There was really little left to prove here. We could eat all summer in this canyon. Great numbers of flowering shrubs promised squaw-apple (*Rhus trilobata*), and red barberries or *algeritas* (*Berberis fremonti*) and chokecherries promised some fruit for later in the year, but a totally wild diet in this area, while possible, would certainly grow monotonous. We stayed out our time, eating well but nothing new. We had to release seven catfish that were surplus. The recycled Coke bottle was a good provider. We arrived back at the camper with bags of biscuitroot, saltbush, and wild onions, but we were ready to seek some less arid part of the West and see what it could provide.

I had a yearning to gather Indian potatoes (*Orogenia linearifolia*) and yampas (*Perideridia gairdneri*), both delicious wild foods I had not tasted in a long time. We headed for the Yampa River Valley in northwestern Colorado. We passed many a promising area as we drove, but resisted the temptation to stop. We couldn't possibly sample the wild food in every section of the West—it's too big a country, and plant habitats are wonderfully varied. I did gather a little

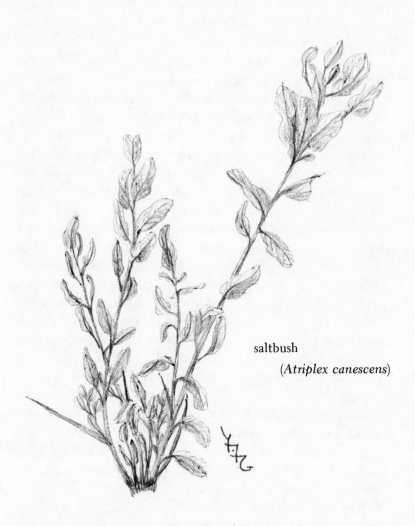

saltbush
(*Atriplex canescens*)

sheep sorrel, purslane, wild lettuce, and cattail hearts to help out with lunch, and then drove on.

It was worth it. The Yampa River Valley is a garden of wild food. The first riverside town we hit was Craig, Colorado, and right in town we found a vacant lot or two covered with dandelions in just the right stage to cook best, plus all the curly dock (*Rumex crispus*) we could ever use. Then we found a great plenty of salsify (*Tragopogon porrifolius*) with roots like slender carrots. These sell on the markets as "oyster plants" and make a delicious root vegetable. We gathered enough of everything for dinner.

The road to Steamboat Springs was lined with cattail marshes, promising great food supplies, but we saw no yampas or Indian potatoes. We took a kitchenette suite in Steamboat Springs and cooked our wild fare on an electric stove. This is one way to enjoy wild food, preparing it with salt, butter, and civilized condiments. You don't have to go on hard-nosed survival trips and see how much you can suffer.

Next morning we consulted the biologist of the local university, Bob Krear. He doubted that we could find the spring sprouts of yampas. He also doubted that the little wintered-over tubers would be good at this time of the year. However, he did know where the Indian potatoes grew. This plant is seldom more than three inches high and, with its slender leaves, it is almost perfectly camouflaged when growing in grass. It can be abundant on a grassy hillside and never be noticed. After Bob pointed them out to us, Mike sat down where several were growing and gazed at them for about ten minutes. He discovered the secret. His eyes became trained, and he could see great patches of Indian potato where the rest of us could see nothing but grass. We had our training sessions and were soon digging up the tiny tubers in great numbers. Each tiny plant bears but one tuber, and it is usually only one-fourth to one-half inch in diameter, though we did find one giant 1¼ inches in diameter. They

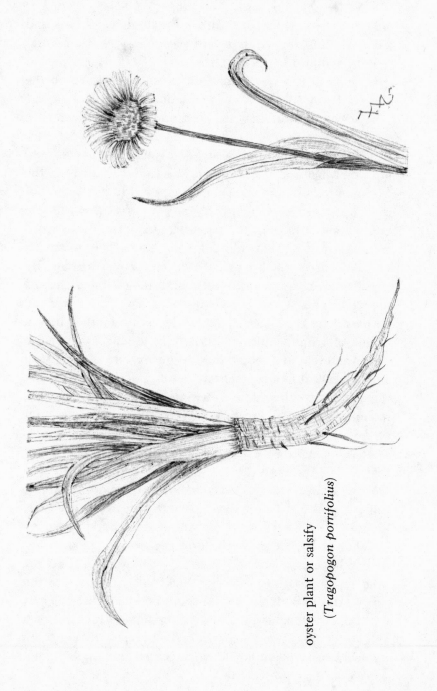

oyster plant or salsify
(*Tragopogon porrifolius*)

are tedious to gather, but worth it. Raw, they are crisp and palatable; boiled they are utterly delicious, one of the finest root vegetables I have ever tasted. We laid in a good supply.

In our fruitless search for yampas we even drove up the Yampa River to the town of Yampa, Colorado, but the valleys were mowed hay meadows and the mountains were still covered with snow. We gathered a great many delicious dandelion crowns, more salsify, and found winter-over rose hips that became our standard tea-timber, replacing the Mormon tea of Utah. In Yampa we talked to Mr. Jensen of the Forest Service, a man who eats yampas every fall. He kindly showed us, on the map, where he gathers his supply, and told us where we could camp near there. This involved a sixty-mile drive on dirt roads, and on the way we saw five mule deer, a dozen marmots, and innumerable ground squirrels. The stockmen of this area have killed off the coyotes, lynx cats, eagles, and hawks, and now they have a plague of ground squirrels eating up the range. They were everywhere about the campsite when we arrived, so David and Mike went ground-squirrel hunting and shot several with their small, 22-caliber rifles. They are excellent meat animals, resembling the dark meat of chicken in flavor. It takes a lot of them to make a meal as they are small.

At the campsite we found another species of biscuitroot that was a little better than the ones we had been eating in Dolores Canyon in Utah. Dandelions were plentiful at the camp site. We left Freda and Mike to prepare dinner while the rest of us started upstream to find other food resources.

While walking slightly ahead of the group I spied a large porcupine eating grass in a little meadow. Signaling the others to approach cautiously I ducked down by the streamside and got a large cottonwood between me and the creature. This enabled me to sneak up unnoticed until I was able to cut the porcupine off from the timber and safety with one wild rush. A porcupine would never place at Belmont:

they can make about two miles an hour going downhill with
a favorable breeze. Even while rushing out to head the
porcupine off, I noticed that the little meadow was overgrown with winter cress (*Barbarea verna*), an excellent wild
relative of cultivated cabbage.

That evening we had a large stew made of dandelion
crowns, biscuitroot, both tops and roots, winter cress, ground
squirrel meat, porcupine liver, some of our precious hoard of
Indian potatoes, and wild onions. Next day we started for
the yampa grounds, three miles away and several thousand
feet above. It was a strenuous, tiring walk in that altitude but
breathtaking, for it was superbly beautiful country. Elk
droppings and elk tracks were everywhere, and a series of
beaver dams formed giant stairs up the stream. Finally we
puffed our way up to the aspen groves where yampas were
supposed to flourish.

We did find a few last year's yampa stalks, but the tubers
that I had hoped would winter over and be better than ever
in the spring were no more than hollow husks. My desire for
yampas became an expedition joke, and Colleen and Mike
started calling me Granpa Yampa. Now I knew I would not
find yampas this trip. The disappointment was tempered by
finding a great patch of Western spring beauty, which has a
tuber that rivals a potato and tops that make one of the
finest of wild salads or cooked vegetables. While digging
these, Colleen's nose found tiny, grassy, wild onions with a
fine flavor. As our supply was already used up, we welcomed
them. Then Mike found the strings of tubers under the
Western chickweed, and we began to fill our bag. Who needs
yampas? As my hunger grew I kept remembering that huge
porcupine carcass soaking in salt water. Tonight we would
eat red meat like proper savages. On the way down, we
stopped by a beaver dam and gathered a load of rhizomes of
cattails that seem to flourish at any altitude, longitude, or

latitude if they can find a little water in which to wet their feet.

On arriving back in camp we prepared our underground oven, using water-sprinkled bunchgrass for a steaming agent. We put in the porcupine, the spring beauty tubers, and the Western chickweed tubers. While these were cooking we gathered young stinging nettles for a vegetable. Colleen and I harnessed the stream in a little rock dam and made it clean the cattail rhizomes. Freda found a patch of wild mint and used that, the spring beauty tops, and the tiny wild onions to concoct one of the best salads ever tasted. While waiting for the porcupine to cook and the nettles to boil, Mike and David went hunting and got six ground squirrels. We planned chicken-fried ground squirrel for breakfast.

To our hungry crew the oven-cooked porcupine was as delicious as a roast goose. The tubers were done to a turn. The young nettles made a grand vegetable, and, with the delicious salad and some cups of rose-hip tea, we voted this the best meal of the trip. Afterward we roasted cattail rhizomes over the campfire, peeled them, and ate the starchy interior. It is as good as sweet potato but does contain fibers. With a blazing campfire to dispose of the fibers we found them no handicap to our enjoyment. It was better than a marshmallow roast.

The next day we had our fried ground squirrels for breakfast, then found a new treasure near the camp. Burdock was just shoving its first, tiny, folded leaves through the spring ground. Digging below these betraying signs we found mighty, starchy burdock roots, more than an inch in diameter and more than a foot long. Here was food in great quantities. We boiled the roots with what was left of the porcupine. At this altitude water boils at a lower temperature, so it took three hours until the roots were tender, but they proved worth the wait and the work of gathering all that wood. The Japanese have long treasured burdock, raising it in their gardens, but we consider it a worthless weed. It is really good when gathered at the right time and properly cooked.

Late that afternoon we changed our campsite to an area where jackrabbits were reported. It was a high, sagebrush flat, with practically no wild vegetables. There were green plants but they were mostly lupines and death camass, both poisonous. I managed to shoot one jack, and David shot another.

The next day we moved back to our Indian potato patch, and planned a feast. We dug the largest quantity of Indian potatoes ever assembled in modern times. (I have this fact on Mike's authority, since he dug more than half of them.) We found more Western spring beauty tubers and tops for starchy vegetable and salad. Then we finally got the nerve to dig some of the bulbs of the glacier lily, which was just coming into bloom. This is a grand wildflower and an excellent food, but the use of them as food could lead to their extinction if they are taken indiscriminately.

They tend to grow in clusters, too thick for their own good. A cluster can be improved by judiciously removing a few lilies from the very center. Also, one must earn this right by planting at least two bulbs in good places for lilies to grow, thus starting new clumps for future use and beauty. By observing these rules we got a dozen bulbs apiece for the crew, along with the leaves and even the flowers, for these are good, too, and would make a tasty addition to the salad we planned. We even took some of our old friends the biscuitroots—not the roots this time, but just the peppery, celery-flavored foliage and stems—for the salad.

I boned the two rabbits and cut the meat into stew-meat sizes. People who don't like jackrabbit usually dislike the flavor of the meat when cooked with the bones. The bones impart a jackrabbity taste, but the meat cut from the bones before cooking is one of the finest of game meats. We concocted a great stew of this meat with Indian potatoes,

spring beauty tubers, salisfy roots, and glacier-lily bulbs. It
was a fine stew, especially when eaten with dandelion crowns,
the gorgeous salad of spring-beauty tops, glacier-lily tops and
flowers, and biscuitroot tops. Again we ended with cattail
rhizomes and felt that the West had fed us well.

The next morning we tried to go to even higher altitudes
but found them still under snow. By unanimous vote we
decided to adjourn the journey until warmer weather. I went
back to Pennsylvania and stayed until after the great flood
that Hurricane Agnes spewed on us, and then went to
Albuquerque to pick up Mike and Colleen. This time Freda
was unable to accompany us. I am no match for the wiles of
children, especially those of my own grandchildren, so I took
their mother, Pat, along with me as an ally. We drove to
Gallup, and while we were there the greatest flood in
Gallup's history ravaged the town. We were able to get out
the next day, drove to Rough Rock, Arizona, where I have a
friend, Douglas Dunlap, teaching in a Navajo school.

David Hiser, the *Geographic* photographer, arrived and we
drove up to the top of Black Mesa, just in time for another
flood. I was beginning to feel like a Jonah. After the
cloudburst let up, we found great fields of Rocky Mountain
bee plant. This plant, a member of the Caper family, has
long been useful to the Indians of this area. When young and
tender it is cooked and enjoyed like spinach. The leaves are
sometimes cooked for a long time, then strained, and the
juice cooked down until it is black and almost solid. This is
dried and is a double-use product. It can be dissolved in
water and eaten in time of food shortage, or it can be
dampened and used as a black paint to decorate Navajo clay
pottery.

Perhaps the most important use of bee plant was as a
grain. It seeds copiously, and the seeds are large enough to
make gathering them worthwhile. One Indian source says

that they are best when one grinds one cup of bee plant seeds
with two ears of corn. Do they mean two large ears of
modern corn, or two of these tiny ears that we found in the
cliff dwellings? Unfortunately, the seed wasn't ripe enough
for us to try this, and the plant was apparently too old to be
good cooked like spinach. We did try that, and, while it
might interest a very hungry man, we found it pretty hard to
take. It was very bitter, aromatic, and with a bit of the scent
of goat. We did find several species of lamb's-quarters,
growing in great profusion, all of them delicious just boiled
and seasoned. We also found the spiny shrub called *Tomatillo*, bearing a bumper crop of orange-colored berries.
Tomatillo means "little tomato" and they do taste a bit like
the tomato, except that the seeds are a bit more bothersome.
We enjoyed them raw, in salads, and cooked, and with the
addition of some orange juice, they were delicious.

Next morning we went back up the mesa road, stopped
along the way to gather Mormon tea and piñon tea. The
piñon tree bears the justly famous pine nut, one of the
sweetest and finest of wild nuts. They are very important to
the Indians in the years that they produce big crops, but,
alas, a big crop only comes about every five years. When I
was a boy we gathered the clear, golden, hardened drops of
resin from the trees and used it for chewing gum. In a
one-room school I attended in New Mexico as a boy,
everyone in the school chewed piñon gum except the
teacher, and he chewed tobacco.

The piñon is the most fragrant of all the pines, and a tea
made by pouring boiling water over piñon needles translates
that fragrance into taste. We gathered a supply for future
use.

I have been experimenting with methods of getting
drinking water in deserts. Maybe that's why floods follow me
around. But what do you do when floods fail? A great deal of
rain can disappear into pure sand dunes and leave no trace

that it has ever been there. There was an extensive dune area near Black Mesa. We drove there to set up a solar still.

To make a solar still you dig a hole. Place a container to catch the water in the very center of the hole. Stretch a piece of clear plastic loosely over the hole and cover the edges with the dirt you dug from the hole. Place a rock on the plastic directly over the container inside. This pulls the plastic down, making an inverted cone with the apex directly over the container. The sun shining through the clear plastic, striking the opaque earth below, sets up a hothouse effect and makes the hole beneath the plastic much hotter than the outside temperature. This evaporates water from the soil which condenses against the cooler plastic, which is made cooler by the outside temperature. These condensed drops of water run down the inverted cone to a point under the rock weight and drip into your container. The container can be partly buried to keep it cool enough so the water doesn't just re-evaporate. This device has worked well for me on Maine islands, changing saltwater into fresh, but I seem to have trouble with it in deserts.

We dug down about two feet and stretched our plastic in the late afternoon. The next morning we came by, and the container had a cupful or so of water in it. We decided to leave it for a few more hours and see how much more water we could cook out of this sand. Meanwhile we experimented with yucca, about the only plant that flourished on the dunes. We knew that yucca was eaten by some ancient Indians. They also used the fiber for weaving, and the root as a soap substitute. We found that a cake of this wild soap would produce a little lather when rubbed very hard in soft water. This is reputed, by the Navajos, to make a hair-restoring shampoo. If you dispute this they merely ask, "Have you ever seen a bald Navajo?"

We found that the bases of these sharp leaves would make a good spoon to eat beans out of a can. One can also split away most of the flesh from the leaf, leaving the spine intact; remove the fleshy part of the remaining strip of leaf, leaving the fiber; give the fiber a twist; and have a wild needle and thread to sew up the rents in one's clothes, made by the spines of yucca in the first place. In the very heart of the yucca we found that the bases of the yet-unborn leaves were edible and tasted pretty good eaten with beans shoveled in with a yucca spoon. Colleen found that she could split a leaf into pliable sections with her thumbnail and weave little mats from the strips. We have already mentioned that yucca bloomstalks are edible, if you stretch the definition of the word edible. The immature fruits are eminently edible, tasting a bit like squash when cooked. On at least one species, *Yucca baccata,* the ripe fruits have a thin layer of sweet, edible pulp, a food highly valued by Indians and by those whites who knew a good thing when they tasted it. I learned to love this fruit as a child and can testify to its palatability. Truly, yuccas are wonderful.

We went back to our solar stills and found little more water in them than we had observed earlier. We all had a sip of solar-distilled water, and, outside of being a bit warm, there was nothing wrong with it. Mike, a very practical boy, wanted to know why one didn't merely carry a container of water into the desert rather than carry all the gear to make a solar still.

On this trip I was determined to get into really high mountains, above timberline, higher than I had ever been on the ground. Backpackers frequently ask me how they can find wild food above timberline, and I had always answered by saying, "Go to a lower altitude." But I wanted to know what was really up there. The San Juan Mountains, in Southwestern Colorado offer the easiest paths I knew into this high country. These mountains were mined extensively for gold, silver, and other valuable metals until rather recently, and the roads used to take the mining machinery up the mountains still exist. They are not good roads; indeed, they will scare the pants off any timid person, but they can be traveled by jeep by a cautious and careful driver who also has unlimited courage. Pat seems to have those qualifications. I don't, but I'm not saying which ones I lack. When we rented our mountain-climbing jeeps in Ouray, Colorado, I turned the driving of the vehicle over to her.

We made good time—seven miles the first hour and a half. That's the kind of roads they were. We didn't stop until we were well above the timberline. In July the mountains were one huge, magnificent flower garden. The scenery was unbelievably beautiful. A whole meadow of rose-colored blossoms finally brought us to a halt. They were wild onions (*Allium geyeri*), acres of them, growing at 12,000 feet. We laid in a supply and felt better about the possibility of a wild dinner. These high-altitude onions were the finest flavored of any wild onion I have ever eaten; they're even good raw if everyone in the party eats them. These onions can be used for more than a condiment. They contain a rather high percentage of sugar and would make an excellent survival food for injured climbers or lost hunters. Of course there is always the danger that any rescue party who found you might refuse to carry you out. We all ate wild onions, then drove on up the mountain leaving a trail of onion odor behind us.

From the top of a minor pass we saw Ptarmigan Lake below us. It is really just a beautifully clear pond, fed by the melt from surrounding snowfields, with many little green meadows nearby. We unanimously selected this as our alpine campsite. We drove down and parked our jeeps at the upper edge of a snowfield several acres in extent. At the bottom of the snowfield was a little meadow where we pitched our tents. Colleen and Mike called the snowfield "the down escalator." They would load some gear on a piece of plastic, then leap on it and slide down to the campsite. I even tried it myself. Sliding down snowbanks can be great fun on the twenty-second of July.

Our tents were pitched on wild food plants, for our little meadow was covered with Western marsh marigold and American bistort. The white-flowered marsh marigold is very plentiful on these mountains and doesn't just grow in the marshes as does its Eastern relative. On a hill back of camp I found two kinds of biscuitroot, one a white flowered species and the other with yellow blossoms. Then I found mountain sorrel (*Oxyria digyna*) in unlimited abundance. The little round leaves of this plant are sharply acid with a good flavor. They are excellent when mixed with the leaves of the Western marsh marigold (*Caltha leptosepala*), and when cooked with sugar these sour little leaves taste as good as rhubarb.

Then we made the big find, alpine spring beauties growing, not in the fertile meadows, but, among the most barren-appearing rock slides. They stand only about three inches high but the spatulate leaves are thick, fleshy, crisp, juicy, mild, and delicious. One can eat the whole top, leaves, flowers, and all. The roots are huge, an inch in diameter and up to a foot long. One does not dig these roots. They apparently grow without soil, so one can merely lift away the loose rocks surrounding them until the root lies exposed. The slightly spongy texture of the root put me off until I tasted it. It is one of the finest root vegetables I have ever eaten.

There was high-protein food available also, but we agreed not to use it. The ptarmigans that give Ptarmigan Lake its name were so tame one could approach within a few feet of them. They will fly only if forced to, and then with loud squawks of objection. They are large as a bantam chicken, varicolored at this time of year, and one ptarmigan would make a sustaining meal in emergencies. However, they are part of what gives this alpine country its fascinating charac-

alpine spring beauty

(Claytonia megarrhiza)

ter, and though they seemed plentiful we decided to let them continue to decorate the landscape. Other decorations were the coneys, or pikas, we saw scurrying over the rock slides or peeking with beady eyes from under the rocks. They resemble small, short-eared rabbits when seen from a distance. These are much shyer than the ptarmigans and would have to be shot or snared if one needed them for food. Our emergency wasn't all that dire, and we were so enamored of this strange mountaintop world that we wanted to do nothing to disturb its charm.

We had brought up a jeepload of wood and a campfire was burning in the meadow. Pat was calling for her wild cavemen to bring in some food. One of our reference books said that Western marsh marigold was too bitter to be used for food, but I suspected the writer had tried it in midsummer at low altitudes. The Eastern marsh marigold, *Caltha palustris*, is also too bitter for food at that time, but is delicious if gathered in very early spring. Here we could choose our seasons. Out on the bare knolls it was early summer. In the meadow at the foot of the snowbank it was late spring. Only a few feet away, at the melting edge of the snowfield, it was earliest spring. I gathered my *Caltha* just as the first leaves were being uncovered by the melting snow, cooked it with a bit of mountain sorrel to give it a vinegar flavor, and it was excellent. The spring beauties and a few more leaves of mountain sorrel made a beautiful and delicious salad. Colleen discovered the best way to cook spring-beauty roots, dicing them up with a few wild onions, wrapping them in aluminum foil, and roasting them in the coals of the campfire. These little packets of goodies were so popular that she soon used up all the roots we had gathered. She merely substituted the leaves and flowers for the roots and these were almost as good.

While the marsh marigold had proved much better than advertised, the American bistort (*Polygonum bistortoides*) didn't live up to its recommendations. It was exceedingly abundant in this high country, showing its thin-stemmed white-to-rose flowers, which the local people call "Grandma's wig," in every available piece of soil. The leaves are good when cooked like spinach, but they can't compete with mountain sorrel and alpine spring beauty. The roots are shallow and folded, and not too hard to get, but the first batch we boiled tasted like alum. We later found that if all older sections of the root were removed the remainder made a passable starchy root food. Our conclusions: It would make an excellent emergency food if mountain sorrel and alpine spring beauty were not around.

All this food-gathering sounds easy when one says it fast, but the altitude was affecting me, and every four out of five minutes were devoted to merely trying to breathe. I could walk only a few dozen steps until I had to stop and puff. The others were affected less, and Pat didn't seem to be affected at all. She's a born mountaineer. The thin air seemed to engender a lassitude that was hard to overcome. Fortunately our food plants were so abundant that we needed little time or effort to gather all we could use.

It became obvious that a person who knows wild food plants could survive the short summers of this alpine region with little or no food from the outside. A backpacker could bring in salt, sugar, cooking oil, some protein concentrate, and eat luxuriously and nutritiously from the wild plants until the snow covered the food plants. We gathered some of the marsh marigold, mountain sorrel, and alpine spring beauties to take with us when we left two days later, for these are goodies not likely to be found at lower altitudes.

We were not going much lower, for we wanted to sample the foraging at timberline, which here is about 11,000 feet. What a difference that 2,000 feet made! It was another world, botanically, and, best of all, my breathing was back to normal. I could actually run up a hill. There were still snowbanks in north hillsides a few hundred feet above us, but spruce groves alternated with flowered meadows all around. All our camps in this area had running icewater from the snow melt. We felt more at home in this area, but were still overflowing with the awe and wonder of the mountaintop. Our alpine experience was not for sale or trade. It had been a tremendous happening in our lives, one that we would never forget.

Here we found another species of broad-leaved dock with leaf petioles up to two feet long. Peeled, these tasted like rhubarb. The wild seems to furnish many rhubarb substitutes in the West. Whole fields of wild onions invited us to give our breaths a wild, primitive aroma. Fireweed, both the low and the high, offered good vegetables. These would have been better earlier in the year, but boiled in two waters and flavored with butter and salt they were still acceptable. The marsh marigold we brought down from the mountain was found to be very good when cooked in a cream sauce. Two kinds of edible sedum grew here, one called king's crown and the other called queen's crown. These can be eaten raw, as a salad, or cooked like spinach. They don't compare with alpine spring beauty in either category, but were perfectly edible. Biscuitroot offered its familiar root vegetables and salad. There were clumps of garlic mustard growing along the stream. The flavor reminded us of spectacle plant we had eaten in Utah.

But best of all we found abundant fields of yampas, the plant we had sought so long. The tubers were still a bit young, but approaching full size. They were delicious raw, better than the sweetest carrot ever eaten, and cooked they were superb. Now we understood why Indians had occasionally battled one another for the right to gather this fine food plant in certain areas. After a big dish of boiled yampas I felt fulfilled. I had finally earned my name, Granpa Yampa.

Here we also tried cow parsnip. I had long heard that this giant relative of the carrot was edible, both the roots and the top, but the evil smell of the plant had always driven me away. Here they stood higher than our heads in some wet ravines. The smell of the roots could still make one feel a bit ill, but the peeled upper young stems were quite good, tasting like very juicy celery. The roots are reputed to "taste like rutabagas only not quite so good." I think we would almost agree, for I heartily dislike rutabagas and consider anything worse inedible. The smell persisted through cooking, and no one could stand the flavor of the roots. However, the peeled, upper stems chopped into short lengths and boiled were much like stewed celery. They were perfectly acceptable.

Our next move was to a very picturesque abandoned ranch at about 10,000 feet altitude. There were some cleared meadows and pastures surrounded by aspens. Just above the aspens grew a forest of spruce, and we could look up the mountainside and see where the spruce forests ended and the snowfields began. A blind man could aimlessly snap a camera in this country and get good pictures.

Around the tumble-down log houses and barns of the abandoned ranch headquarters, lamb's-quarters, dandelion, and nettles were abundant, and in a nearby field wild rhubarb grew rampantly, probably an escape from an ancient garden. This expedition seems haunted by rhubarb and rhubarb substitutes. Pat showed off her ability as a camp cook by contriving a cake of biscuit mix, sugar, canned milk, and powdered eggs, which she managed to bake to a turn in an aluminum cooking pot with the lid covered with coals, in the manner of a Dutch oven. Covered with rhubarb stewed with sugar we enjoyed a partially wild shortcake.

Here we made Indian digging sticks of slender aspen saplings sharpened to a chisel point and hardened in the campfire. Then we went after dandelion roots. These high-al-

titude dandelions had roots as large as carrots, and they were
not bitter at all. Indeed, they were voted one of the best root
vegetables we had eaten on the entire trip. The digging sticks
worked well, but quickly became dull. We soon found we
could easily resharpen them by holding them in the fire until
slightly charred, then rubbing the points on a convenient
sandstone.

There was a giant, yellow-flowered thistle growing in the
fields and clearings, but the large flower stems were already
too tough to eat. They would probably be excellent earlier in
the year. Alerted, we soon began finding first-year rosettes of
the same thistles, which had enormous tender white roots,
like long carrots. Here was substantial, good-tasting food.
We dug a great quantity of them.

We spent the evening washing and paring our haul of
roots. We finally spread our sleeping bags under the stars,
and enjoyed hearing and seeing the many owls that haunt
that neighborhood. I had never seen so many owls at the
same time.

The next morning we drank some rose hip tea and went
gathering again. This time we took lamb's-quarters even
though it was covered with green buds, and it turned out to
be quite palatable when boiled, buttered, and salted. It
probably contained more food value than the young, tender
plants usually eaten. We also donned heavy gloves and
gathered nettles. These made a delicious vegetable when
cooked like spinach. These and our roots made a good
brunch, one of our best wild meals, and our last one.

Before leaving home I had made a list of the edible plants
I had expected to find in the areas where I expected to be. I
had found most of them, and also quite a few that I didn't
have on my list, but one I especially wanted to try was sweet
cicely (*Osmorhiza obtusa*), which grows in partial shade of
forest glades. As we drifted slowly down the road, leaving our

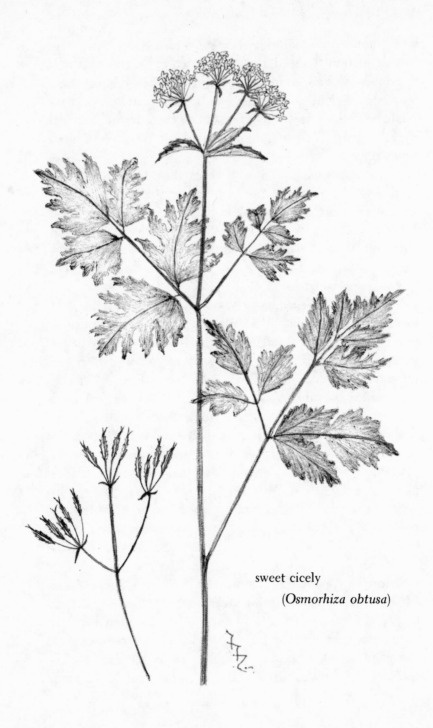

sweet cicely
(*Osmorhiza obtusa*)

last camp very reluctantly, I kept my eyes on the vegetation we were passing. Then I saw red baneberry, which is a beautiful but poisonous plant. I love this plant because it keeps good company. I knew that wherever it grows one is likely also to find sweet cicely. We stopped and searched, fruitlessly at first. Then I started to collect a specimen of a plant I couldn't immediately identify, and, while my spade was in the ground, I saw a sweet cicely right beside me. I called my crew and had them train their eyes on this plant, then spread out and hunt. Everyone was soon yelling at the top of his voice. The plants I was seeking were plentiful in the area, but they so closely resembled the lush vegetation surrounding them that we had been unable to see them.

The children went wild over the sweet anise flavor of the tiny green fruits that grew at the top of the sweet cicely. The whole plant smells and tastes like anise. I dug some roots, peeled them and we enjoyed a delicious snack of this beautiful plant. It was a fit ending for a fine trip.

3. You Can Go Home Again

FOR AN eater of weeds and gatherer of wild herbs, December may seem a poor month for an expedition, but that partly depends on the direction in which you go. I had long had a hankering to revisit that strange little corner of Texas where I was born, but my longing was mixed with fear. Did this country that lived so vividly in my memory— where I had first learned to feast off nature's free offerings of wild food—really exist, or was it just a persistent daydream of a childish mind? Nearly fifty years had passed since I had been there. Even if such a place had existed then, would it be recognizable after a half-century of change?

I am related to many people in Red River County, but I didn't know just how many. I had met very few of these relatives over the years. I had trouble understanding their dialect and could no longer speak it at all. I was afraid that I would feel more like a stranger among my own people and in my native land than anywhere else on earth!

My mother wrote that she would be spending the yearend

holidays with her eighty-six-year-old brother in Clarksville, and asked me to come down and become reacquainted with my relatives. With my mother and her wonderful memory to guide me through the maze of uncles, aunts, and cousins by the dozens—and all their in-laws and outlaws—I decided to go.

I was encouraged to find that there was no airline service to my home town. I landed in Paris, Texas, thirty miles away, and was met there by a cousin I had never seen. When we drove into Red River County, the calendar rolled back fifty years. The land I remembered was still there, almost totally unchanged. It was actually wilder now. The cottonfields and sharecroppers are gone, replaced by fat beef cattle on lush pastures. But this is not the Texas of popular imagination, with broad plains, cactus, and mesquite bushes. This is wet country, with bogs, creeks, and rivers. It is timber country, with tall pines in the upland, sandy sections, and lowlands such as creek bottoms covered with oak, hickory, wild pecan, black walnut, elm, maple, box elder, sycamore, and sweet gum. Sawmills whine and buzz. Botanically, this area is more closely related to the Central Atlantic States than to the rest of Texas.

That evening there was a gathering of the clan to greet the returned wanderer. As my mother explained the relationships to me, I felt I had more connections than a telephone switchboard. I had met very few of these people before this night, but I was "kinfolks" to them and therefore no stranger. It was the first time I can remember being in a crowd of my own relatives. I felt secure, protected, loved— and somehow corporate. The people became real, the dialect not only became understandable but began to fit itself onto my tongue.

But how about the land and the wild plants I had first

loved? Could they be brought back to life in midwinter? The next morning I loaded my cousin's car with minnow net, waders, a camp cooking set, and a spade. For a companion I took along my cousin's little daughter, who had been a fan of my books and is well on her way to being a wild food freak. We took along some butter and a little salt and drove into the country.

I easily found my grandfather's old place. A slight depression where the rainwater cistern used to be was the only sign of a long-gone house. The plants hadn't changed. The blackberry vines appeared to be the same ones that I had gathered wild fruit from when I was a boy and from which my grandmother made crusty cobblers topped with thick cream from the springhouse. Along this fence we had gathered wild poke and mustard greens, and in that little meadow (seeming much smaller now than it did then) we had picked wild strawberries. Down a slope was the old bottom field where I learned to catch a huge red crayfish that built mud chimneys among the young corn plants. Just beyond is Boggy Creek where my grandmother showed me how to catch sunfish, perch, and catfish. In those days fishing was woman's work.

Boggy Creek was low, no more than a series of shallow pools with barely a trickle running between them. I donned the waders and dragged the minnow net across the pool. I netted no fish, but I did have a half a dozen large red crayfish wriggling in the net. This crayfish (*Procambarus clarkii*) is so big and delicious that it has been called the "land lobster." A few more drags through a few more pools and we had more than the two of us could eat.

On the field side of the brush that lined the creek we found black haws (*Viburnum prunifolium*) still clinging to the bushes. The little fruits are mostly seed and skin, but what pulp there is is as sweet as a date. My cousin's daughter and I each filled a pocket with the dry fruit to nibble as we went along, spitting the seeds in likely places so more black haws could grow.

In the corner of the old field I found four small persimmon trees, where I had remembered only one large one. This evidence of immortality gladdened me. The soft, sweet persimmons were still hanging, waiting to be carefully picked to avoid being squashed. Wild pecan trees still had reluctant nuts in the half-opened husks. We threw sticks into the trees and enough nuts rained down to give us a good supply.

Then we came upon a hackberry tree crowded with hard red berries. It was very near here, under a hackberry tree now long dead, that I invented my first wild food recipe. When I was only five years old, I shelled some hickory nuts and pounded them in a cloth with some of these sweet hackberries, squeezing the resulting sticky paste into a ball, then unwrapped and ate it. It was a wild candy bar. We have hickory nuts and hackberries in Pennsylvania, where I had tried the same trick. The result was so poor that I thought it must take a childish taste to appreciate this delicacy. But when I tasted the hackberries from this Texas tree I knew what had been wrong with my recent attempts. These berries were ten times sweeter than those from Pennsylvania trees. We gathered the dried berries in a bag.

A patch of brilliant green drew us, and I soon identified this lush growth as the winter rosettes of the finest edible thistle that grows, *Cirsium altissimum*. The prickles on these winter leaves are as soft and tender as the rest of the leaf. The fat, white roots were as large as organically grown carrots. We gathered one bagful of the tops and another of the roots. We detoured on our way back to the car to examine the old spring that had furnished water for my grandparent's house. There wasn't a trace of the old spring-house, but where it had stood was now a lush bed of watercress. We filled the rest of our bags.

Soon we were driving down a narrow road to Sulphur Bottom, a jungly wilderness, miles in extent, where wild boars still roam through growth so thick and dark that the owls hoot at noon. We came to Sulphur River, where I once caught the largest catfish I had ever landed. We drove across a rickety bridge, up a long slope, topped the rise, and were in another land. A broad prairie lay before us, the beauty marred by dozens of oil wells. We felt like strangers, out of place. Almost in panic, I turned the car around, recrossed the river, and felt no ease until I was again safely wrapped in Red River County.

We turned off at a faint dirt road that led to a beautiful spot beside a clear spring. Here we built a fire and boiled some crayfish and thistles. The huge crayfish tails, first shelled, deveined, and then eaten with melted butter, were more delicate and delicious than any crustacean I had ever tasted. The thistle tops were a mild—and excellent—cooked green vegetable, and the white roots, which cooked perfectly tender in ten minutes, were superb, resembling artichoke hearts in flavor. This plant is closely related to the cultivated artichoke and the family resemblance is obvious to the taste buds. The watercress, eaten as a salad, gave just the right pungency to brighten the mild foods. The persimmons were soft, sweet, and luscious, and at my small companion's insistence we planted the seeds in strategic places near the spring for her future reference.

Next, we shelled pecans, cracking them between two stones. We put carefully considered amounts of the shelled nuts and sweet hackberries into my neckerchief, then I pounded and ground them between the stones into a gooey, thick paste. We squeezed this paste into the shape of a candy bar, then unwrapped it and shared the natural sweetmeat.

As I sat by the fire, sharing this joyful experience, I knew that the land and the life it nurtures accepted me, welcomed me home. I had loved many places, and never left any place without regrets. There are bits of my heart and the small children of my spirit in many far corners of the earth. I had no idea that this strange little corner of Texas was going to have such a different impact on me. But here the very dust is partly composed of the bodies of my ancestors. Their bones lie under this ground. This land formed them and they formed me. I am tied to this country, and to its people, with bonds I cannot loosen. I have come home.

4. The Western Underground

I T WAS a Navajo Indian who first told me about the bush morning-glory (*Ipomoea leptophylla*) when I was a boy in New Mexico. I was walking on some sand hills along the Rio Salada, a river with a wide bed but only one tiny stream of salty, alkaline water across which I could easily step. I saw the Indian coming, riding a little pinto mustang that looked scarcely able to carry its rider and the heavy, homemade Indian saddle. The Indian's long hair was done up in a hank behind his neck and wrapped with red yarn. He wore a beaded vest, moccasins trimmed with silver buttons, and carried an ancient Winchester across his saddle in front of him.

The Navajo reined in to rest his pony and pass the time of day. He spoke no English, and I spoke no Navajo, so we conversed in the faltering Spanish both of us could manage. I conveyed to him that I was looking for wild plants that were good to eat. After recovering from his astonishment at finding a white boy interested in this subject, he became very helpful, tying his pony to a chapparal bush and walking about with me, showing me the plants that his people considered good food. It was still fairly early in the spring, but he stopped by the scraggly, silver-leaved buffalo berry bushes and explained that the berries were *"muy bueno"* in the fall. He pointed out three kinds of cacti that bore edible fruits later, all "very good."

Then he began talking about some weedy-looking dried stems that grew in abundance along one side of the dunes. He pointed out the young plants just coming up from the old dead centers, and kept pointing down talking about *"muy bueno por comer"* (very good to eat). Finally, as he saw I didn't get it, he stooped and dug in the soft sand with his hands, saying it was very deep. He was describing something but I still couldn't comprehend just what. At one point I caught the word *papas*, a local Spanish idiom for potato, and the word *palo*, another colloquialism meaning shovel. So I gathered there was some kind of tuber down there, but I couldn't believe his sign-language description. He was talking about something as big around as his thigh and as long as his leg. He made me promise to get a shovel and dig. With a last warning that it was very deep, he rode off.

It was only a short distance back to our camp, so I returned for a shovel. I selected some plants on the side of a dune, figuring if it was all that deep it might be easier to tunnel in from the side rather than go down from above. This proved a good guess. I soon struck a large root still going straight down. The sand was easily shoveled, so I followed the root down for almost three feet. This monstrous tuber the Indian had described was rough, dark, misshapen, and some seven inches in diameter at the top. I dug to the right and left of the hole I had already made and got two smaller roots, one about three inches in diameter and two feet long, and another about two inches across and over a foot long.

I cut into these with my pocketknife and found white,

somewhat succulent flesh inside. The largest one was woody and hard to cut, but the smaller ones were tender. I cut a slice from the middle-sized one, removing the rind, and took a bite. It was crisp, sweet, and quite palatable, a little like raw sweet potato. I threw the big one back into the hole, covered it, and took the two smaller ones home.

We peeled off the dark outside rind, sliced the roots thinly, and started experimenting. Fried slowly, in a covered skillet, for at least forty minutes, the slices were excellent, sweet, and a bit softened, but not at all mushy or mealy. They stayed whole and were even a bit crisp. Boiled for an hour and a half they were good, but the water seemed to have soaked out some of the flavor. They were also still crisp and whole.

The bush morning-glory is found along the eastern edge of the Rocky Mountains from South Dakota to Kansas and west to Montana and New Mexico. Its stems are erect, branching, and may reach a height of four feet, although they're usually much lower. The leaves are slender, from one to six inches long and don't at all resemble morning-glory leaves; in fact, you wouldn't know that this was a morning-glory until it blooms. The blossoms, pink-purple to rose in color, and darker in the funnel part, are the typical morning-glory shape. Since a single root will furnish so much food, this is a good plant.

About ten years ago I again found myself in the West, this time driving with a friend from Denver to Salt Lake City. It was still winter in the high mountains, but as we dropped below the snow line we began to see signs of spring. When we stopped to explore a sawmill and logged-off area, a small boy from the mill appointed himself our guide. He led us over an open, gravely area, reached down and pulled up a tiny plant with a root about the size of a radish attached. He rubbed this on his trousers and then ate it. Then he told us this was the Indian potato and showed us how to recognize the little green leaves just appearing, as well as last-year's seeded plants.

Obviously an umbellifer related to the carrot, the dwarf plant stood no more than six inches high and produced round roots up to an inch in diameter. Alerted, we filled our pockets with them. They were crisp, mild, and good eaten raw, with a carrot-parsnip-parsley flavor that was easy to take. That night we scrubbed our loot with a pot cleaner, then boiled them. They were delicious with butter.

How could I have overlooked such a good plant for so long? I readily identified it in a botanical manual as *Orogenia linearifolia*. The common name was given as Indian potato, but nothing was said about its edibility. Nowhere in the wild food literature could I find a word about them, and yet they were well known at the sawmill. I finally found reference to this excellent wild food plant in two recent books. What's more, I found that it is fairly widespread in Colorado and west to Utah and Washington. People there may be missing a good thing.

Another underground food of the West is one that I have never mentioned before—for the simple reason that I didn't know it existed. It's another plant that has largely escaped the attention of workers in the wild food field, called the Western chickweed or starwort (*Stellaria jamesiana*), and it is closely related to the ordinary chickweed that grows so freely in our fields and gardens. The irony of it is that, as soon as I saw an illustration of this plant in *Edible Native Plants of the Rocky Mountains*, by H. D. Harrington (University of New Mexico Press, Albuquerque), I recognized it; but I had never known that it bore edible tubers. I remembered seeing plenty of these plants on my father's ranch in northwestern New Mexico.

The next time I went that way I made sure to look for it.

Although it was November I had no trouble locating some of the plants; in fact, a few skinny, frostbitten ones were still trying to bloom. The sparsely branched stems were eight to sixteen inches long, very weak and spindly. The leaves—unlike those of the Eastern chickweed—were long, thin, straplike, and two to four inches long. Tiny white flowers were five-petaled, with each petal appearing to have had a bite taken out of the outer end. I found them growing near the bottom of an eroded mesa where scrub oak trees and the sagebrush met in sandy loam. The water pouring off the sandstone mesa probably gave this area extra irrigation during every rain, and as a result, the nearby sagebrush was tall and lush.

I turned up a few of these chickweeds with the shovel to find that the tubers were really swellings on one root, and there were several of these swellings strung together like beads. Selecting a few of the largest, I washed them with a little water from my canteen and tried them raw, with the peel still on. They were crisp but easily chewed, sweet, and had a spicy flavor all their own. How many times I would have welcomed such a food supply as I rode over these same hills as a boy! If I had only known what to look for I could have found food wherever I happened to be.

Later, I tried these little "tubers" fried, baked, boiled, and added to stews, and liked them in all guises.

These three plants far from exhaust the good underground foods of the West, but you may not be too familiar with them. Once you learn to recognize them in all stages of growth and dormancy, you can dig the underground, edible parts any time of the year, except of course in areas where the ground freezes very deeply in winter. You Westerners, get out and enjoy some of these fine wild foods, but don't take them all. I am beginning to get the urge to go on another Western foraging expedition.

5. A Wild Survival Challenge in Arizona

SEDONA, ARIZONA, is more than a euphonic name—it is a very real place, and near it is Verde Valley School, a coeducational preparatory school that actually uses the environment as teaching material.

And what an environment! Red-rocked mesas and buttes; desert areas complete with cactus, yucca, century plant, mesquite, and catclaw; hills covered with piñon and juniper trees, lofty mountains with ponderosa pine forests and well-watered canyons with trout-filled streams, lined with sycamores, black walnuts, hackberries, and wild grapes; Indian reservations with some of the most primitive and culture-rich aborigines left in the United States.

Nearby are Mexico and the unspoiled shores of El Mar de Cortez, usually shown as the Gulf of California on U.S. maps. And within a short radius of the school are literally hundreds of Indian ruins, showing the great population that this arid land supported in prehistoric times.

Here Verde Valley School teaches natural sciences in the

tremendously varied life forms that surround it: geology in the deeply eroded canyons where the history of the world is exposed; anthropology among primitive Indians; and ecology out in a place where it is easy to see how all life forms are interrelated and how easily man, in his ignorance and arrogance, could destroy this beautiful land.

My opportunity to visit this unique educational institution came from its director, John Huie. I first met John when he was assistant director of the Minnesota Outward Bound School, and I was there teaching ecology and survival. We were drawn together by a mutual interest in creative outdoor education. I think John wanted to challenge me now. He knew what I could do in the lush wild food areas of Minnesota and Ontario, but he wanted to see if I could get by in Arizona in midwinter.

I had done my homework before I went out there, and I knew a little about how this dry country had managed to feed so many Indians. I arrived during Project Period—when the school suspends regular classes and allows the student to pursue special interests—and many of the students had chosen to learn how the ancient peoples of this land fed themselves. Beyond an initial introductory lecture, I never taught in the classroom. We found out how the ancient Indians ate by going out in the hills and eating the same things that they did.

The first plant we explored was the century plant that exists in the millions in this part of the country. It is known in Spanish as mescal, and one tribe of Indians, the Mescalero Apaches, take their name from this plant, so important was it in their nurture and culture. They used its fiber to weave cloth, its leaves as thatch for their houses, many parts of it as food, and its sap as their national beverage.

The first thing I had to explain to the ecology-sensitive students was that conservation could not be equated with non-use. The century plant exists in such abundance on the hills of northern Arizona not despite the Indians' use of it, but *because* of that use. If a century plant is correctly gathered for food it immediately saves and multiplies its life by putting up four to eight sprouts from its base. The more you take, the more there will be in future years—if you know how to take it.

The century plant can furnish food any time of the year, and when I was there the starchy heart was the prize. The Indians gathered this by sharpening a heavy pole in a chisel point, then running at the plant and driving the chisel-edge deep into it between the lower leaves, finally prying out the heart with the upper leaves. The students and I had fun making an equivalent tool of a heavy iron driveshaft, heating it in a hand-bellows forge and beating it out on a makeshift anvil. After experimenting to learn just where to thrust it down into the plant, it worked wonderfully.

When the center of the plant is pried out and the outer foliage removed, it leaves a heart—or perhaps it would be better described as a "head"—from the size of a large turnip to the size of a cabbage, which is almost solid starch. All records I could find indicated that the Indians always cooked these great balls of food long and slowly. I wondered why. These same records said this food was nourishing, but fibrous, and around the old underground ovens in which the Indians cooked it, one could find balls of spit-out fiber. Our first agave head was tender, crisp, and white near the center, with a flavor that reminded me of a coconut heart. It seemed an excellent salad plant, but we discovered why it needed to be cooked. That initial good flavor was deceptive, and in a few minutes our tongues and throats were burning unmercifully.

Boiled for about two hours, it tasted a bit like summer squash, only more substantial. Fried long and slowly, it was better than fried potatoes, but the best way of all to cook it was the way the Indians did it. We dug a pit, lined it with stones, built a hot fire, and heated the stones white-hot. Then we covered the bottom and sides of the oven with century plant leaves, laid in the starchy heads, piled on more leaves, then covered everything with dirt and forgot about it for two days. The old reports said that these leafy hearts came from the oven scorched and black; ours looked very much as they did when we put them in, but were cooked soft to the very centers. This slow, dry heat apparently transforms much of the starch into sugar, for these were sweeter than roasted sweet potatoes.

Cooking in any way apparently completely removes the century plant's tendency to sting the tongue, for we noticed no discomfort while eating it. Nor was the heart or head fibrous, as we had been led to believe. But we did discover where those chewed-up balls of fiber came from. The Indians cooked this food wholesale in great pits up to fifteen feet across, then removed the top leaves, crushed the tender head, and dried it in the sun to a sort of hard, sweet bread, which was a great trade item among the Indians of this region. As we removed those top leaves from the roasted heads, we saw that each one had a tender, white base where it joined onto the head, something like an artichoke leaf, and this leaf base is fibrous. Obviously, the frugal Indian workers were saving the fiberless hearts to make into trade bread, while subsisting on the fibrous leaf bases, which are not bad food at all if you don't mind inelegantly spitting out balls of fiber.

The oven-roasted agave heads were so good that I decided to try making a chiffon pie of them, following a recipe for pumpkin chiffon pie. It was creamy, light, and utterly delicious; some of the enthusiastic students declared it to be the best pie they had ever tasted. I'm sure it would also be good prepared like candied sweet potatoes. Here is one Indian food that the paleface will also find palatable.

The starchy head does not exhaust the century plant's usefulness. It spends years (though seldom a century, as the names implies) in building up this great ball of food in preparation for expending a vast amount of energy when it finally blooms. When the bloom stalk finally appears, it may be up to a foot in diameter, and if allowed to grow will do so at the rate of about six inches a day until it is fifteen to twenty feet tall and covered with orange flowers. But the Indians seldom let it grow. While the vast stalkbud was still shorter than the leaves, they socked their wedge-shaped poles down its side and pried it out. This was also roasted in an underground oven, but was more a green vegetable than a starchy breadstuff. Actually related to asparagus, it is probably the largest asparagus-type sprout in all nature.

The plant went right ahead with its strange chemistry, turning the great store of starch into sugar and pumping the cavity left by the removed stalk full of sweet juice which would ferment into a mildly alcoholic drink in one day. In good years the Indians could carouse for months on this *pulque*. After the Europeans came, the Mexicans learned to distill this juice into tequila and mescal—and there is nothing mild about these drinks. I once met a man in bad shape in Tucson who had just returned from Mexico. He said he had tried two drinks down there, one called "to-kill-ya" and the other called "must-kill-ya," and they almost had!

We didn't spend all our time on the century plant. Also very important to the early Indians was the prickly pear, *Opuntia* species. Even in mid-December we still found some of these with ripe fruit. There are many species of this cactus, with fruit of varying quality, but the two species we found bearing in winter were both purple-red in color. One was quite sweet, while the other was a bit tart. The sweet ones—with the stickers brushed off with a handful of grass, then carefully peeled to make sure none of the tiny bristles found their way onto the tongue—were a delightful fruit. The sour ones made an excellent jelly. Even when these plants are not bearing fruit, they can still furnish food. The young stem joints, usually called "leaves" by laymen, can be trimmed of their clusters of stickers with a sharp knife, then roasted or boiled to make a mucilaginous vegetable with considerable food value.

The beanlike fruit still hung on the honey mesquite trees. The seeds were ground with corn by the Indians to make a nutritious bread, but the chief source of food from the mesquite bean came from the pulpy pod, which has a pronounced sweet flavor. We found that we could mildly enjoy chewing on these pods, but none of us were actually enthusiastic about them. I'm sure that they are nutritious and energy rich and would certainly interest a really hungry man. Even the Indians apparently had a higher regard for their food value than for their flavor, for they ground the pods into a fine meal, stirred this in water, and drank it down in as few gulps as possible.

Other Indian foods were better appreciated by the students. Ground cherries, *Physalis* species that closely resemble those growing wild in Pennsylvania, grew in many nooks and crannies. I suspect that these were actually cultivated by the ancient Indians of this region, but now they are thoroughly wild. They make a wonderfully versatile food, being good fresh or dried, as a dessert or salad material, in jams, pies, or cooked with peppers and meat into savory dishes. And I have no doubt that the Indians of Arizona once cultivated the canyon grape, *Vitis arizonica*, for I saw them growing in rows near Indian ruins. I know they also appreciated the little Southwestern black walnuts, *Juglans rupestris*, that grow along canyon bottoms, for we found the cracked shells in many a shallow cave in the area. We managed to gather quite a few of these small black walnuts. They are much

mesquite

(*Prosopis juliflora*)

smaller than our Eastern black walnut, but they shell out rather easily and are very flavorful.

We came to the conclusion that there was no need for anyone to go hungry in central Arizona at any time of the year. Before I left the students had formed a Survival Club, which plans to sample the wild food straight through the year.

6. Bald Island Revisited—
And Loved Again

WHEN THE call of the Maine coast became irresistible last August, I returned to the Outward Bound School on Hurricane Island in Penobscot Bay for a few weeks. Outward Bound is an inspired educational movement, but its wise director, Peter Willauer, realizes that a school is only as good as its teachers, so he has literally scoured the earth for inspired ones.

Outward Bound is not an academic school with instruction coming out of the instructors' notebooks and into the students' notebooks—without making an impression on either. Its textbooks, classrooms, teaching material, and examination papers are the sea, boats, islands, forests, shores, tideflats, and all the rest of that wonderful complex that makes up the incomparable Maine coast. In response to current trends, a few coeducational courses are now available.

Each course consists of at least six "watches," with twelve boys, ages sixteen to twenty, to the watch, plus two of twelve men, one from the twenty to thirty bracket and one from the thirty and upward. The course is rugged and demanding but well within the capability of any healthy man or boy willing to give it his best. To one who has been used to teaching from books in classrooms, the learning rate is astounding. In the short twenty-six days, the boys are taught Seamanship and Navigation, Boat Handling, Sailing, Drown-Proofing (I doubt that a boy who has received this instruction could drown himself even if he tried!), Fire Fighting, Emergency Care including resuscitation, Rock Climbing, and the course in which I am most interested, Ecology and Survival.

Although the majority of the staff are Americans, there are specialists and watch officers from England, Scotland, Wales, and Australia, for these countries had Outward Bound Schools long before they came to America. Together they form a competent and congenial team of the most dedicated teachers it has ever been my pleasure to meet. They have to be dedicated, for Outward Bound is a non-profit organization and cannot pay high salaries. It is largely supported by donations from foundations, corporations, and individuals who believe that our modern young people are in desperate need of the kind of instruction and experience that this school offers. It is not just for rich men's sons, for half of the student body comes on scholarships.

I helped to set up the course in Ecology and Survival in 1965. My first Outward Bound job was a tough one. I had a yacht and crew at my disposal and was told to cruise among the Maine Islands, going ashore on uninhabited islands, that had been loaned to the school for their Solo-Survival Program. The object was to see whether or not they had sufficient wild food to support a series of boys, each staying three days. This job was a good example of the drudgery and hardship that can be involved in a naturalist's life.

At first I was skeptical of the value of Outward Bound training, but that was only because I misunderstood its purpose. I thought it was to jerk adolescents into super–he-man adults, and I wanted no part of a masculinity cult. I am always a little suspicious of the real masculinity of men who have to constantly demonstrate their ferocious maleness.

But that is not what Outward Bound is about. What it really does is to bring the student into better and more meaningful relationships with nature, with himself, and with his fellow students. It gives him knowledge, tools, and attitudes so he can make the most of these improved relationships. It works as well with girls and women as it does with boys and men. In the Minnesota Outward Bound— where they use the wilderness and canoes instead of the sea and whaleboats—they have as many girls' and women's courses as they have courses for men and boys. I can personally testify that the gentle sex is a joy to teach in these areas.

At first it was hard to get enough really eager students, but now Outward Bound is better known and they have more applications than they can handle. The physical requirements are not hard to meet—the student's own doctor must certify that he is able to take strenuous exercise without harm, and that's about all. The chief criterion used in selecting students is their own eagerness to take this course. A father may be thoroughly convinced that this is exactly what his son needs, but unless the boy shares his dad's conviction he is likely to prove a dud.

The new eco-environmental awareness that is sweeping our land has had a beneficial effect, and now there are much better attitudes. The teaching was really hard work—some-times four classes a day with a lecture in the evening. Usually the first half of each class period was devoted to gathering wild foods; during the second half we cooked and ate them under the same conditions the boy would find when he went out to his own island.

With all that exertion I found no difficulty in eating four extra meals a day and still doing justice to the meals served in the school dining room. I would often finish up the evening by cooking and eating some crabs or clams, opening a few sea urchins and spreading the delicious orange-colored roe found inside on some crackers or French bread. This rounded out a good eight meals a day—that's living.

I found the boys full of apprehension about the solo-survival test when they arrived at the school—but by the time training was finished they were all eager to get on those uninhabited islands and try out their new skills. They did a good job, and, after three days of lonely communion with nature on a diet which nature furnished, they came off those islands walking ten feet tall.

The solo was finished about mid-course, and I found myself without classes. I was given a motorboat and told to inspect the solo islands to see if the intensive use to which the school had put them had resulted in any damage. After supporting a series of about thirty-five hungry boys for three days each over the last five years, the islands remained almost completely unchanged. There were a few trails worn from clam bed to berry patch, but even wild animals will do that. The seafood around the islands was still as abundant as ever at low tide, and the shores were still nature's vegetable gardens. The raspberries, blueberries, and wild strawberries were as sweet and abundant as ever. Boys who have been trained to live in harmony with nature, rather than trying to conquer her, do not destroy.

I reserved an entire day to inspect just one of the islands. It has an area of only seven acres and could be adequately inspected in thirty minutes, but this little hunk of soil and granite, called Bald Island, is where I did my own three-day solo five years ago, and I love every inch of it.

There is a little protected harbor with enough water to keep a deep-draft boat afloat at low tide. This part of Maine has pretty tremendous tides. The first things that struck my eyes on going ashore were the rose hips (*Rosa rugosa*). It had grown wild around the edges of this island, and the shrub thickets were decorated with thousands of huge, red rose hips, all larger than plums, some more than two inches in diameter. I could have picked a dozen bushels if I had use for so many. I did have use for a good many, for each soft hip—split in two and the seeds raked out—furnished several delicious bites of nature's finest vitamin C concentrate. That's the way I like to get my vitamins, in good-tasting food, rather than pills.

I slowly circled the island at high-tide level, greeting with gratitude each plant that had contributed to my well-being when I dined on them years ago. At low tide I again circled this farther shore and satisfied myself that all the familiar seafoods were still there in abundance. I inspected the ancient quarry, now a freshwater marsh, drank from the cold spring, climbed to the top of the island's one hill, sat down, and dreamed a dream.

What a place for a hermitage this island would make! I love the tiny islands that I can encompass—chase life into a corner, examine its web and weft, and see how it is woven. Someone once lived here—there are the remains of a burned-out house standing on the grassy isthmus between the two hilly ends of the island. The bricks in the old foundation could be used again. A warm, snug house, designed to blend into this rugged inland landscape, could be built here with little expense. The spring would furnish all the clear, cold, pure water—unchlorinated and unfluoridated—that one could use. The shores were covered with driftwood that could be used for fuel, and every storm would renew the supply.

When the tide is out—the table is set. These shores furnish clams, mussels, sea urchins, crabs, tiny eels, and huge periwinkles, all you could use. The waters are swarming with fish and lobsters. I caught four mackerel, one large tautog, one sand shark, and two large sculpins in one evening's fishing from a steep foreshore. Out in the deep channel that separates Bald from an adjacent island, one could lay a long line and catch a doryload of cod, pollack, hake, and haddock in a few hours.

Along the upper shore there is a regular garden of vegetables. Orach, a relative of spinach, but fleshier and milder, grows in great abundance. Glasswort, a crisp, translucent salad plant, covers part of a tide flat. Sea blite, good raw or cooked, abounds. Sea rocket, a member of the mustard family with a horseradish flavor, is to be had in any quantity for the picking. Strand wheat, a grain as valued in Iceland as wild rice is here, grows in all sandy spots. There are great patches of beach peas, a bit tedious to shell but tasting like good garden peas. An abundance of sheep sorrel could furnish piquant acidity to salads and soups. The burdock growing on the isthmus, mostly around the remains of the old house, could yield leaf stems that can be prepared like stewed celery, roots as starchy as potatoes with more flavor, and peeled flower stems that provide a very palatable and nutritious vegetable.

Cattails in the marsh could furnish succulent hearts known as "Cossack asparagus"; bloom spikes, a mealy vegetable; sprouts white and tender that are excellent cooked or raw; and ropy rhizomes with a starchy core that tastes like a sweet potato. There are even a few maples from which you could make your own sugar.

Not only are the fruits of this tiny isle delicious and

plentiful, there is an amazing variety. A wild sweet cherry grows near the old house. There are abundant patches of wild red raspberries, blueberries, wild currants, wild gooseberries—and in the marsh I discovered bog cranberries and mountain cranberries growing within a few feet of one another, both in abundance that couldn't be depleted by a whole family. Wild strawberries cover a hillside in spring. All this, besides the endless quantity of the finest rose hips I ever tasted.

Do you yearn for domestic vegetables from your own organic garden? There is an acre or so of arable land on this island, plenty to provide for a family, a milk cow, some pigs, and enough chickens to keep you in eggs and fryers. Near where I sat there is a nesting area used by seagulls, eider ducks, cormorants, and guillemots, and bird manure is over a foot deep. There are thousands of tons of rockweed available at every low tide, and, when a bit of the salt is washed from it, it makes a mineral-rich mulch. Are you too lazy to hose out the salt? Then gather it only after a heavy shower.

Have you been so spoiled by civilization that you must have power to run labor-saving gadgets? Why not build a picturesque old Dutch-type windmill on the hill where I sat and let this calm breeze generate nonpolluting power against its sails to pump your water, grind your grain, shred your mulch, and run your gadgets. You could even charge batteries to run one of the nonpolluting, noiseless, little electric outboards to power your dory.

I really drew a pretty picture of what life on this island could be like, but it was on the sand and the incoming tide washed it away. The island is not for sale, or I would have owned it long ago.

7. When the Tide Is Out —The Table Is Set

THERE is something utterly fascinating about a small island. Large islands won't do. To keep one conscious of its islandness it must be small enough to walk around it in an hour. It must also be fruitful. There is a bit of Robinson Crusoe in us all, and an island must be able to feed us or it won't qualify.

There are whole constellations of such islands on the drowned coast of Maine, and one of the best of these is called Little Garden, an appropriate name. Best of all, the owner of this beautiful island is a friend of mine.

We did not set out to prove that a family shipwrecked on one of these islands in summer could survive. These little islands offer wild food in such an abundance that mere survival would be no problem. We wanted to prove that a vacationing family could live intimately, creatively, and nondestructively on one of these islands, feasting on the free food that nature offers and enjoying doing it.

Our own boys are long grown and gone, but Freda and I

have excellent child-credit with many parents, so we merely borrowed a family. We were lucky to get Mark Fulford, seventeen, and his younger brother, Jonathan, ten, for both these boys have been on such expeditions with us before, and they are skilled and enthusiastic wild food gatherers.

We had to take potluck on girls. My friend, Bill MacFee, of Vinalhaven, Maine, was making the arrangement for our stay in that area. Bill thought he could rustle up a couple of Girl Scouts who would enjoy such an adventure. With the photographer this would make seven people, nearing over-population for a food-gathering tribe on a twelve-acre island.

When we drove off the ferry at Vinalhaven, we were met by our friends from Outward Bound and by Bill and the two girls he had selected. The girls were two pretty eleven-year-olds with charming personalities and Down East accents, but they seemed to know very little about the plants and creatures of that area and had little desire to learn about them. They admitted to being very fussy eaters and were full of apprehension about trying new foods. We were a bit dubious, to say the least.

We landed on Little Garden at low tide, near noon, on a foggy Monday that threatened rain at any minute. We ate our last civilized food in the boat, then sent the leftovers away with the boatmen. We were on our own. I took a perverse pleasure in the challenging apprehension I always feel when I know that I must adapt to nature, and do it now, or I will go hungry.

I could see beds of blue mussels (*Mytilus edulis*) on the rocks at waterline. The incoming tide would make them inaccessible in an hour and the next low tide would be at midnight. I ran across a narrow neck of the island and was filled with exultation when I saw the clam beds I remembered were still there, and bountifully populated with delicious steamer clams (*Mya arenaria*). I set the two boys to gathering mussels and digging clams while the rest of us carried our gear over the jungle of seaside granite and pitched camp on one of the few level places on the island.

The girls and I set off around the island to find some plant foods to go with our clams and mussels. Bayberry (*Myrica pensylvanica*) grew all about our campsite. The fresh leaves are a fine herb to steam with seafood, and they make a fragrant, delicious tea that can perk up a meal no end. A few hundred yards around the shore we came on a wild garden. Orach (*Atriplex patula*) and sea blite (*Suaeda maritima*) grew so low on the beach that they would be lapped by the highest tides. They are both relatives of garden spinach and chard and can be eaten raw in salads or cooked as greens, and they come ready salted.

Just above these, in the debris tossed up by past storms, grew a patch of beach peas (*Lathyrus japonicus* var. *glaver*) loaded with green peas in their prime. The peas are borne on thrust-up stalks that seem to be asking you to gather them. These peas look and taste like undersized garden peas. Although they are crowded in the shells they are a bit tedious to shell because of their small size, but time we had.

Among the peas grew still another food plant, sea rocket (*Cakile edentula*), a member of the mustard family with a mild flavor of horseradish, delicious in salads or as a sauce for seafoods. Just above the wild garden was a wild orchard—a great patch of wild rose (*Rosa rugosa*) with rose hips large as plums, but only a few dozen were ripe enough to eat. The whole clearing was filled with red raspberry canes (*Rubus idaeus*) just coming into the prime of ripeness. Both these fruits boded well for the following days, for the season would outlast our stay here.

My elation was tempered by the reaction of the girls. They refused to taste of any of the foods we found, even those delicious red raspberries. They were willing enough to help

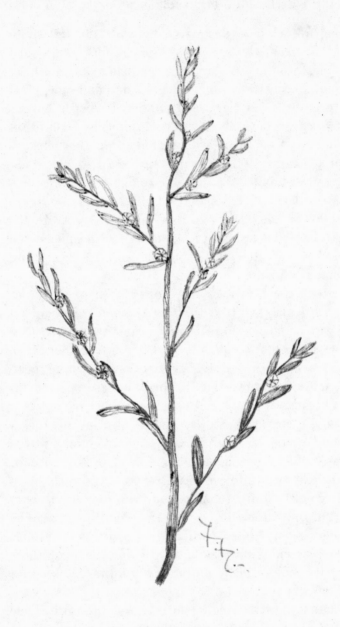

sea blite

(*Suaeda maritima*)

gather them, but made no attempt to learn to recognize anything, asking each time they reached for a leaf or fruit if they had the right plant. I saw trouble looming.

Our dinner was totally from the wild; steamed mussels, bayberry tea, boiled peas, a rocket and orach salad, and fresh raspberries. I have dined worse in some pretty fancy dining rooms. David, the photographer, Johnny, Freda, and I found it very satisfying, but Mark had trouble with steamed mussels and tried to make a meal on the vegetables and fruit, while the girls would eat nothing but one spoonful of familiar-looking peas. They had an acute attack of homesickness and went to their tent and had a good cry. I turned gloomy and so did the weather. We retired to our tents in fog and drizzle. I had planned to awaken Mark, Johnny, and David at midnight for a low-tide foray on a rocky reef, but when my alarm went off the rain was beating down on the tent and the sleeping bag was snug and warm.

We arose in fog and rain. The girls were red eyed from crying themselves to sleep, Mark had found his vegetarian dinner inadequate and had lain awake thinking of steak dinners, Johnny had caught a depression from the girls and said he had felt sick during the night. But Freda, David, and I were thriving. We had steamed clams, bayberry tea, and hot clam nectar for breakfast. The girls passed, but the rest of us filled up on hot food and felt better.

We fished the high tide from a steep foreshore where we could cast into deep water, but luck wasn't with us. Johnny caught the only fish, a gruesome sea raven (*Hemitripterus americanus*). This fish looks poisonous but isn't. However, when we cleaned it we found the flesh almost solid with parasites. We threw it away. More clams, mussels, vegetables, and fruit for lunch.

An island is a small body of land surrounded by the need for a boat. I had brought along my SportsPal canoe and a tiny outboard motor, both tested in these waters before, but the motor was stubborn and was being repaired at the Outward Bound School. Mark, David, and I paddled to another nearby islet to see if we couldn't find some change of fare. Things immediately began to look up. The sky cleared and the sea was calm. The new island proved fruitful. The rose hips were riper, the peas more plentiful, the raspberries redder than on our own island. We found two treasures we had not seen on our island. Near one end of the island was a seabird nesting area where bird guano had made the soil exceedingly fertile. There we found luxuriant sheep sorrel (*Rumex acetosella*), which is sharply acid with a lemon flavor. It is the essential ingredient of a gourmet soup and is great raw in salads and just eaten plain with seafoods. In this same area were whole gardens of ripe wild gooseberries.

For lunch we munched our way around the island. On a saltflat we discovered another good one, glasswort (*Salicornia europaea*), which is a succulent, tender, ready salted salad all by itself. We saw dandelions, sow thistle, bull thistle, burdock, and several other plants that would make good food for a really hungry person; but they are a little too bitter in midsummer to be palatable. We were finding food so plentiful that we could afford to be a bit fussy. We left these for an emergency more dire than our own. A castaway could stay fat all summer on this tiny island.

In an old nineteenth-century quarry we found a marsh with a great plenty of cattails (*Typha latifolia*). The base of the plant, peeled down to a tender, white heart, is a sweet, mild, nutritious, starchy vegetable.when cooked and has a cucumber flavor when eaten raw—a very welcome addition to our cuisine. The few patches of soil around the marsh were so covered with bright red mountain cranberries (*Vaccinium Vitis-Idaea*) that they resembled red-flecked carpets. This subarctic fruit is so acid that it is hardly edible raw; cooked with sugar, however, it makes a delicious cranberry sauce.

We had not planned to introduce any supplementary foods into the wild cuisine for another day or so, but the food situation was becoming desperate for the two girls. I broke out cooking oil, sugar, and some flour that we had agreed would be used only for batters, breading, and thickening in cooking wild foods. Fried clams in batter are a totally different gustatory experience from steamed clams. With the clams we had boiled cattail hearts, boiled peas, a very tasty salad of salty salicornia and sour sheep sorrel perfectly dressed with nothing but a little oil, and two desserts, fresh raspberries and ripe rose hips boiled with sugar, gooseberries, and cranberries.

Our efforts were wasted on the girls. They refused to try any food that contained anything that had ever been the least bit wild. They retired to their tent for another cry, and the sky, perhaps in sympathy, began dripping rain. The rest of us were enjoying the food but we were depressed by the presence of suffering children. We decided that the girls, who were crying out that they were homesick for their mothers, should be returned to those mothers as soon as possible.

The next morning, Bill MacFee came by in his boat and agreed to take the girls home. I'm sure they felt that they had been rescued from a fate worse than death. I had Bill run me over to the Outward Bound School to pick up my little motor. There I recruited two new members for the expedition: Sara Bay, a young woman with Outward Bound training, and Charlie Willauer, the twelve-year-old son of the director of Hurricane Island Outward Bound School. Charlie had been following me around for years, as I taught survival to the students, and had come to consider wild food better than anything the supermarket could furnish. Charlie

mountain cranberry

(*Vaccinium Vitis-Idaea*)

brought along his fishing gear and his little outboard boat, promising to relieve the fish famine.

Suddenly, the weather changed, the sea calmed and spirits rose. We were a goodly crew. That evening we built a campfire out on the rocks, below high-tide level. We drank sweetened bayberry tea and formed a little mutual-admiration society among ourselves. We were getting a bit tired of mussels and clams. When one lives on manna from heaven it should always come in at least fifty-seven varieties. Mark and I put the little motor on the canoe and put-putted out to deeper water for a try after fish. Almost immediately Mark caught a three-foot shark, the kind usually called dogfish (*Squalus acanthias*); with that whipping, snapping shark between us the canoe felt crowded. Not too many people know that a dogfish is good eating. We cut Mark's catch into a great pile of steaks and put them in a cool place for breakfast.

An unusually low tide was due at 3 A.M. and we were out on the rocky reefs to meet it with flashlights, lanterns, and pails to contain our catch. It was eerie fun examining the weird life forms uncovered by a nighttime low tide, when creatures don't retreat into deeper water because seagulls don't fly at night. They were no safer from us. We collected mussels and waved whelks by the pailful. Green sea urchins (*Strongylocentrotus drobachiensis*) covered room-sized areas in shallow water. Jonah crabs (*Cancer borealis*) socialized in the shallows. Suddenly we were inundated with food of many kinds. We crawled back into our sleeping bags and napped until the sun was high. The shark steaks were as delicious as swordfish.

We took it easy, the inexorable pressure to keep gathering food temporarily relenting to our plenty. We reveled in the returned sunshine, drying our wet gear, and sunbathing. I opened the sea urchins and found them the best I had ever seen, each shell half filled with the beautiful and delicious orange-colored roe that rivals the finest caviar. Tastes are notoriously hard to describe, but after a tasting conference we decided that raw sea urchin roe has four flavors that are tasted one after another. One first notices a salty taste, followed by a rather intense sweetness. This is succeeded by a seafood flavor, a bit like crab, a bit like lobster, but more like itself; and then, finally, there is a pronounced aftertaste of cantaloupe. This sounds like an ungodly mixture of flavors, but they all blend together into a beautiful harmony. Cooked sea urchin roe loses all these exotic flavors and tastes much like ordinary scrambled eggs, but that is also a food flavor to hungry voyagers. We made sea urchin fritters, fried sea urchin, and a sea urchin stew. This last required the introduction of another civilized food, powdered milk. This stew is made exactly like oyster stew, except that urchin roe is substituted for the oysters. It could drive oyster stew off the market. Sara and Freda gathered a pail of raspberries, I made sorrel soup, the boys went fishing. We wallowed in our wealth.

Mark caught another shark. This time we skinned it, finding the skin came off whole, even skinning the fins and tail. The white meat was cut in slender pieces, battered, and fried, to give us some of the fats and starches our pampered stomachs desired. There was another salad, some cooked cattail hearts, stewed mixed fruit. We ate out on the rocks by a fire, and in joy and security watched a magnificent sunset.

The nighttime low tide was so fascinating that the whole group insisted on rising again, at 4 A.M. Dawn was breaking but the night creatures were still out. This time I tried to stand back and observe my young crew in action. They had changed. Though the low-tide bottom was literally covered with millions of urchins, mussels, and waved whelks, they were careful to take only what we could use, and to disturb the beds as little as possible. When they turned over a rock, looking for crabs and baby eels, they carefully replaced it so the teeming life colony that exists under every littoral rock could go on undisturbed. Even when walking along the upper shore they were careful to step on none of the sea-area plants that had been feeding us so well. There was a new appreciation of food and its origin, and, feeling strong and healthy due to the creatures and plants they had eaten, they had developed a new tenderness toward these interesting and useful life forms.

Despite the number of clams we had been eating, the crew still clamored for clams. They seemed to be habit forming. Again I observed that as they dug clams they carefully replaced the small rejects so the clam bed would have a sustained yield. We wanted big ones because we intended to shuck them raw and have some real fried clams. I opened a bucketful of sea urchins, crushed and strained the roe, and had some eggs for egg batter. As we feasted on fried clams and tea, I heard Mark say he didn't know how he was going to survive civilization because now he felt he had to have a cup of bayberry tea to start the morning.

David's wife was joining us in two days, and we decided to welcome her with a wild party, a real gourmet feast of all the better wild foods we had tried. The boys went fishing and again Mark the Shark, as we had come to call him, lived up to his name. This time he caught a shark with a big belly and as soon as she was in the boat she promptly gave birth to seven babies, teaching the crew in a dramatic and unmistakable manner that these were viviparous fish, bearing live young instead of laying eggs as most fish do. They tossed mother and babies back overboard and they swam away apparently none the worse for a rather unusual maternity ward. The boys finally caught a few pollack and cunner, which proved a welcome change from shark, for our dinner.

Both low tides were now in daylight. We arose at dawn

and putted to another little island for edible seaweeds, which seemed to be in short supply on Little Garden. We found dulse (*Rhodymenia palmata*) and edible kelp (*Alaria esculenta*) by the ton on the low-tide rocks of this new islet. We carefully removed the gritty holdfasts where the seaweeds anchored to the rocks—a slow job. Ashore on this almost timberless little island we found a bird-guano–rich soil bearing millions of wild strawberry plants. We had landed here at the wrong season. There were some huge, ripe, rose hips, plenty of large, tender orach, and another abundant patch of beach peas. We returned to our own island with a boatload of food, spread the seaweeds to dry in the sun, and turned the punt over to the younger, more ardent fishermen.

Trying to eat dulse fresh from the water is like chewing on a salted rubber band. Sun dried, it becomes tender and delicious. It should be chewed long, slowly, carefully, and tenderly, to bring out the flavor. A chemist friend of mine tells me this is because the diastase in the saliva gradually turns the peculiar starch this seaweed contains into sugar; but it doesn't taste particularly sweet. It just tastes savory and good.

On the day of the wild feast I arose at dawn to collect what sea creatures we would need, letting the rest of the crew sleep in. It was glorious out on the reef all alone. How easy it would be for one person to provide all his own food in this beautiful environment. If the relationship with nature was kept ecologically sound there need never be a diminution in the productivity of this area. But too many trying it too often would be disaster. How fragile is the beauty and bountifulness of any natural area, and how little we know of the proper ways of preserving its treasures. What we need are not only more trained ecologists, but a larger number of ordinary people thinking more ecologically.

Our guest arrived on a lobster boat that was pulling traps

in the area, and she showed the right spirit from the start. The lobsterman, Ivan Olson, who was the father of one of the deserting girls, was pulling lobster traps on the way to our island, finding more large Jonah crabs than lobsters in them. When he started to throw the Jonahs back, Cheri, David's wife, asked him for them. It was her contribution to the wild food supply. She was a welcome guest.

The great feast took shape. Charlie and Mark returned from fishing, and as soon as they were in shouting distance we knew they had something to offer besides shark! They had fat mackerel (*Scomber scombus*), the tastiest fish of these, or almost any other, waters. Sara managed to contrive two pies—from wild gooseberries and mountain cranberries— beautifully decorated with ripe raspberries. All day there was activity in camp as we dreamed up new dishes and then created them. Finally the whole feast was carried out on the rocks. We ate until darkness closed in. Freda was forced to part with a contraband box of Wheat Thins, which we spread with urchin roe. These and waved whelks boiled in saltwater were the hors d'oeuvres. These were followed by fried mackerel, steamed clams, steamed mussels, crabs boiled with bayberry leaves, and a grand salad concocted of orach leaves, glasswort, pungent rocket leaves, sour sheep sorrel, cucumber flavored leaves of the bead lily, and thin slices of snow-white cattail heart. There was a fruit salad, too, rose hips sliced in half, the seeds removed and the cavities stuffed with ripe raspberries. Then there were two glorious pies and many cups of fragrant bayberry tea.

The next day the whole crew went after more of those sweet mackerel, leaving Freda and me alone on the island. There was a brisk breeze blowing when they left, but the sun was shining through a haze. About forty-five minutes after they left the wind suddenly increased to gale force. The place they had intended fishing was in safe, protected waters, and there had been plenty of time to reach it before this storm struck, but what if they had motor trouble on the way? The small boat would never live in these seas. What if they were so protected that they failed to realize how violent the storm had become, and tried to return in it? We were in an agony of anxiety for hours. We ate leftovers from the great feast with no appetite. I insisted that we eat. We might need the energy and clear thinking that food could give us. The tide came in and stayed in, piling higher and higher.

I walked around the island because I couldn't stay still, marveling at how high on shore the waves were breaking. Suddenly the wind stopped blowing. The seas still roared ashore, but the air was dead calm. From what had been downwind a few moments before, I saw a black cloud racing down on us. I ran for camp and before I reached it the darkness rolled in like late dusk, though it was still early afternoon. Freda was frantically getting all gear under shelter. We went into the tent and lighted a gasoline lantern. The rains poured down.

We sat there praying for the better part of an hour, then we heard voices outside. I nearly tore the zipper off the tent door getting out. There stood all our crew, soaking wet but well and happy. They all had high praise for the seamanship of Charlie and Mark, who had not only brought them safely through the whole, confused storm, but had contrived to fish through most of it in protective bays.

Mark had, of course, caught a shark. They had philosophically decided that if shark was to be their lot they would see how many of them they could catch. Mark had heard that blood in the water attracts hoards of sharks, so he stabbed the first one in the heart, sliced its gills to keep blood flowing, then fastened it to a line, and threw it overboard. Everybody got a hook in the water and began catching, not shark, but large fat mackerel. They had a tubful of these delicious fish.

We rigged a piece of plastic over the cooking place and I

cleaned and cooked mackerel while the rest of them changed
into dry clothes. Those mackerel were so fat that they could
be pan grilled without any added fat whatever. In fact, there
was oil in the pan when I finished about six panfuls. The
stack of grilled mackerel looked like enough to feed a
regiment, but we cleaned it up, happy, hilarious, and even a
bit silly in our relief that all were well and safe again. Never
mind the rain beating down on our thin, plastic shelter; we
had good food, hot bayberry tea, and one another.

There was little left to prove. Obviously, we could go on
eating, or even overeating, in this fashion for the rest of the
summer. We stayed a few more days, explored another
island, finding ripe dewberries, edible evening primrose, fields
of glasswort, and the best rose hips we had found so far. We
also came upon wild mint (*Mentha arvensis* var. *villosa*),
which made an aromatic tea that was good for a special treat,
but all agreed that for steady going it could not compete
with our bayberry brew.

As soon as I saw the first beginnings of waning enthusiasm
I decided to evacuate. I wanted this to be remembered as a
joyful experience, not a time of drudgery and hardship. I
wanted these young people to know that nature, when
approached in a spirit of cooperation and love, would always
be a friend.

We returned to Vinalhaven in late afternoon and found
motel rooms. We reveled for an hour or two with hot water,
shampoos, razors, and clean clothes, and then went to a
restaurant for dinner. No one was ravenously hungry, and our
meals had been so well balanced that no one had developed
cravings for any particular foods. Several in the party ordered
fried clams.

I had trouble getting to sleep. The bed was too wide and
didn't hug me as it should. Finally, I arose, spread my
sleeping bag on the carpet, crawled in, and slept like a log.

We arose at 6 A.M. to catch the ferry to the mainland. At

that hour there was no place open where we could get breakfast, so we faced the prospect of an hour-and-a-half ferry ride without even a cup of bayberry tea. Just across the road from the ferry slip I noticed a great hedge of wild rose hips and ripe, red, wild raspberries. Our crew simply walked over and had their breakfasts, while the other passengers waiting in line to board the ferry gawked at them.

8. The Sound of Opening Flowers in a Silent Land

IT WAS mid-October when the Canadian Broadcasting Company asked me to come to Ontario to make a film on the wild foods to be found there in late autumn. At first they planned only a studio interview. Then they asked me if I could bring along some wild food to demonstrate. Next they wondered if I would be willing to point out some of the wild foods found at that time of year near Toronto. And finally they engaged a hunting lodge and a film crew—and we wound up having a full-fledged stalking party, followed by a wild meal of native products.

This was a test for me, as I had never been foraging in the southeastern corner of Ontario, and had never even been there so late in the growing year. Although a little hedge-hopping propeller plane wafted me from Harrisburg, Pennsylvania, to Toronto in only a little over two hours, I found it a different world. The leaves were just getting into their best fall colors in Pennsylvania but were almost gone in Ontario. I was met at the airport by three beautiful young Canadian girls and could hardly believe it when they identified themselves as the television crew with whom I would be working. A neighbor once asked my wife if she worried about me going off in the fields and woods with attractive women reporters, but she answered, "Not at all. They will soon learn, as I had to, that no woman can compete for Euell's attention against a wild plant!"

As we drove toward the hunting lodge, an hour away from Toronto, I finally got my attention off the scenery within the car and started studying the wayside vegetation. I spotted huge healthy dandelions, some chicory, wild mustard, and burdock as we raced along and knew I would not go hungry. When we stopped at a filling station I walked around it and found wild oats fully ripe, saw cattails in a low spot, and altogether located fourteen wild foods before the tank was filled and a phone call was made.

We met the camera-and-sound crew at an abandoned farm that one of the television crew was turning into a retreat from city life. She had designed a house that enhances rather than destroys the natural beauty of the area; she called it an ecology house. It was built on the brink of a steep hill with the back a full twenty feet from the ground, supported on creosoted telephone poles so that there would be as little interference as possible with the root systems of the surrounding trees. On one side there was an alcove, specially built to allow a magnificent beech tree to remain, and from a distance it appeared to be growing right out of the house. A balcony at the rear overlooked a steep slope covered with spruce and white birch through which one could see a glint of water from the pond at the base of the hill.

Before the house there was an old field, reaching over a high, grassy hill beginning to be spotted by clumps of spruce that set out to reclaim this land from man's former abuse. From the top of the hill, one had a weirdly beautiful view, looking through a vast field of old brown mullein stalks that gave the landscape a prehistoric appearance.

From here we started our search for wild edibles.

In a meadow greener than the rest of the field I came upon hundreds of the seed stalks of salsify (*Tragopogon pratensis*), which is also called goat's-beard or sometimes oyster plant, from a supposed resemblance between the flavor of the stout root and stewed oysters. These were still bearing the blow-balls, resembling giant dandelion seed heads. This is a biennial, so roots from the second-year seeding plants are worthless, but they alerted me—and in a moment I had fine-tuned my eyes to pick out the rosettes of grasslike leaves of the first-year plants, which are hard to see when growing in grass. These were growing too thickly for all of them to mature, so we liberated a few while thinning the patch, giving the remaining plants room to grow and adding to our wild larder at the same time. The soil was a soft, sandy loam and I soon filled a basket with fat roots in the very prime of edibility.

On top of the hill we found first-year evening primrose plants growing so thickly that they actually overlapped one another, making a solid carpet of green rosettes. These are also biennials, storing vast amounts of food in their reddish, carrotlike roots the first year, and then sending up their seed stalks that bear beautiful yellow flowers the second year. These flowers stay closed during the day, then open rather suddenly, and even faintly audibly, just before dark.

When the evening primrose grows as thickly as it does here, it can furnish two excellent foods. The starchy root is a hearty root food, with a hint of pungency that most people like. But even this pungency can be removed by boiling in two waters, then practically drowning it in melted butter. No part of the plant has been explored for vitamin content, but

common evening primrose
(Oenothera biennis)

with starchy roots it is the easily digested calories and flavor you are seeking, so boiling is no heresy. The central crown of the first-year rosette, with all the old outside leaves removed and nothing left but the tender, blanched heart, makes a grand green vegetable. Some people even like them in salads, but to me they are a bit too pungent to be palatable raw. I like these cooked in two waters, also, even if I am sacrificing some of the vitamins I am sure are there. After all, these wild plants have proved, whenever analyzed, to be so extremely rich in nutrients that one can afford to pour part of them down the drain and still have a more vitamin-rich food than you can get from vegetables sitting for days on a produce counter. We dug another basket of the fat roots and gathered a bagful of the tender green crowns.

In doing this, we were careful to leave as many as could grow and blossom in that area. We found that a few flowering plants had escaped the frost on the hilltop and still had their tightly closed blossoms waiting for dusk. Nearby we found dandelions, some of them mistaking the Indian summer for spring and developing new buds and flowers. Chicory was also making new growth. I had gone root-crazy and dug some of the fat dandelion roots—some as large as good-sized carrots—and took some of the chicory roots also. The latter ones were a bit tough and woody in the upper parts, but the lower root sections and some of the large side-roots were tender and sweet. We also filled plastic bags with the crowns of these two plants, for they are fine, vitamin-packed vegetables.

Where one edge of the field overlooked a lake, we found masses of the fernlike foliage of wild asparagus. There is nothing one can eat from an asparagus plant in October, but the young woman who owned the place was delighted to find that she had an abundance of asparagus just waiting for spring.

The day was so pleasantly filled that, before we realized the time, the light became too dim for photographs. We bundled up against the evening chill and went back to the primrose patch to listen to the flowers open. It proved an almost sacramental rite, more deeply moving than many Quaker meetings I have attended. We sat in absolute silence in this silent land, hearing only an occasional soft "plop" as another flower suddenly unfolded to join our meeting. It was one of the finest experiences of the whole trip, made doubly precious because it could not be captured on film or sound tape.

We went on to the lodge for dinner, then cleaned and refrigerated the wild vegetables that were to be used for the following evening's dinner. Then came long hours of interviewing, an attempt to get a hooting owl on the tape, and finally a night's sleep.

Next morning we were up with the sun, for no precious photographing weather could be wasted. We went into an altogether different type of habitat, along a clear, unpolluted stream. Here we found watercress in unbelievable abundance. The one blight on the landscape was all the dead and dying elm trees succumbing to Dutch elm disease. But even these have their compensations, for on these dying trunks were two edible mushrooms in any quantity we wanted— winter mushrooms (*Collybia velatipes*), with curved stems and orange-brown caps, and oyster mushrooms. Between oyster plants and oyster mushrooms, it appeared that we would have a seafood-flavored dinner.

We gathered cattail sprouts and rhizomes; then burdock roots and dwarf mallow, as well as more dandelions and chicory. As we moved nearer to town we came across what was a grand surprise for me—ground cherries—and not the kind that had been reported to grow this far north, but

Physalis pubescens, with its large, yellow, husked fruit. We gathered a pailful, a real boon, because I was beginning to think I'd have to resort to the abundant wild apples for dessert.

Then it was back to the lodge, and on-camera dinner preparation. Since the lake outside the lodge had failed in its duty to supply trout for our main dish, I made it a vegetarian meal, except that I cheated a little by parboiling the oyster mushrooms in beef consommé, then dipped them in beaten egg and cracker crumbs, and fried them as vegetable oysters. The oyster plant really tastes much more like an artichoke heart than it does like an oyster, so it was served as a luxurious boiled vegetable dressed with butter sauce.

Even without the interfering cameras, lights and microphones, that dinner would have taken a long time, for I was cooking far more dishes than there was room for on the stove. The evening primrose roots and crowns were cooked separately. The roots and crowns of dandelion and chicory were cooked together. The tough chicory and dandelion roots were roasted until dark brown and crisp, then ground for coffee. The watercress had all stems removed and was tossed with halved ground cherries, which are even better than cherry tomatoes in a salad. We had the ground cherries two ways, for I also made a two-crust ground-cherry pie with a flavor slightly resembling apricots. The winter mushrooms were a fine delicacy when the brownish skin was peeled off and they were sautéed in butter. The chicory-dandelion coffee was hot, bitter, and actually did taste a bit like coffee. Some of the guests thought it better than coffee. The whole meal was highly appreciated and pronounced an unqualified success.

It was nearly midnight when we finished eating, but this had given the young woman director time to think up new ideas, so I was kept under light and camera and talking into a microphone until 3 A.M., when finally an aging naturalist, groggy with fatigue, was allowed to go to bed.

Ontario in October is certainly not a very stiff challenge to a wild food gatherer, for nature seemed to be spilling surpluses all over the place. But it is a grand area to explore, with a hospitable natural beauty, especially during a spell of balmy Indian summer weather.

9. Stalking in the State of New York

A LUSHER or more bountiful foraging area would be hard
to find than the Finger Lakes Region of New York.
Anyone who goes hungry around there needs either more
knowledge or the energy to use it!

While I found only one plant in this region that I had
never encountered before, I did some kitchen research and
discovered new ways to use three familiar plants—so, while I
went there to teach, I also learned.

My job was leading nature walks for people attending the
Friends General Conference, held that year at Ithaca College. I enlisted the help of a young neighbor of mine from
central Pennsylvania, who knows and appreciates wild foods.
The first thing we did when we got to Ithaca was to locate
some good areas for the walks. This proved no very difficult
task, for any unmowed area around the campus looked ready
to furnish enough different kinds of interesting plants to
serve as teaching materials for the entire week we were there.

One of the most conspicuous wild plants of the area was

the course, rough, jointed charlock or wild radish (*Raphanus raphanistrum*), growing up to three feet high, with stems thicker than your finger. I've known this plant a long time but was always unable to find much use for it. Although a close relative of our garden radish, it doesn't produce an edible root. Sometimes I've added a few leaves to a mixed wild pot of cooked green vegetables, but they're rather rough and hairy, quite bitter, and generally unattractive.

My friend and I took a closer look at this plant. The yellowish buds that would soon be golden, four-petaled flowers were just showing. We decided to try these bud-clusters cooked with broccoli, but first tasted them raw and discovered that they had a delightful pungency like the hot mustard usually served with Chinese food. These would perk up otherwise dull salads and sandwiches. Finely chopped and mixed with butter, they made a complete sandwich spread, better than most herb butters I have tasted. Cooked, the buds were edible but nothing to brag about.

Breaking those thick stems near the top of the plant where they were newly grown, we found them tender, solid, and succulent inside, with a rather rough cortex that peeled off easily. The peeled stems were a translucent green, tender, juicy, and mildly pungent. They would make a good addition to a tossed salad. Boiled only five minutes in salted water, then seasoned with butter, they made a palatable cooked vegetable.

A wild carrot, or Queen Anne's lace (*Daucus carota*), grew everywhere. I make some use of the stringy little carrots this plant produces, mostly to give a familiar flavor to wild stews and vegetable dishes. But the roots must be gathered in late fall or early spring to be much good. This was the last week in June; the first-year plants were so tiny their carrots were thin as fish line, while second-year plants had woody, fibrous roots and were growing three feet tall, getting ready to bloom. My friend idly broke off one of the tender, upper stems about three-eighths of an inch in diameter and peeled off the cortex, as we had done with the charlock stems. Some people think carrot foliage is poisonous because cattle and horses refuse to eat it, but this is merely because of the strong, aromatic flavor these animals dislike. We tasted the peeled green stem and found it tender and crisp—while the aromatic flavor wasn't gone, it had been tamed down to a remarkably palatable level. Also present was a pronounced carrot flavor.

My friend, David Benner, who is a gung-ho health food freak and vegetarian, liked the taste of raw peeled stems better than I did. That aromatic flavor was fine as a nibble, but after eating several raw stems I began to suspect that it wouldn't wear well for the kind of hearty eating I like to do. We gathered a supply and boiled them in salted water for ten minutes, then buttered them—this I dig. I was elated to discover that I could add a carrot flavor and a delicious aromatic herb to wild stews and vegetable dishes at a time of the year I had formerly considered it impossible. I will be observing those wild carrots with a great deal more love and respect than I have accorded them up to now.

Horseweed, compass plant, prickly lettuce, and wild lettuce (*Lactuca scariola*) are all names for one of the most common of field weeds, which is also found along roadsides, in waste places, and nearly everywhere. The leaves tend to arrange themselves with the edges straight up and down and pointing east and west—hence the name "compass plant." The lower part of the plant and the midribs of mature leaves are covered with weak prickles. The sap is milky, as in mature garden lettuce. Indeed, most botanists think that our garden lettuce was developed from this plant. When the young plants first emerge in the spring, they form little rosettes of tender leaves which resemble a yellow-green dandelion except that the leaves are not cut so deeply but are rather wavy on the margins.

I find these very young plants one of the most palatable of all green potherbs. They are a little bitter to use in salads, although my friend David can eat them by the plateful with some chopped onions and an oil-and-vinegar dressing. I like to fry a couple of slices of bacon in an iron skillet, remove the bacon, and dump in a great many of the greens with only the wash water that clings to them, stir them around until they are evenly coated with bacon drippings, then cover the skillet and let them steam for about one minute. Served with a little vinegar and the bacon crumbled over the top, I can easily make a meal of them.

This wild lettuce was in great abundance around the campus of Ithaca College, but it was long past the stage when I usually gather it. Some horseback riders passed, and I noticed the horses were trying to snatch a mouthful of this plant as they went by. We wondered if the tiny, newly grown leaves at the very top of the plant could still be used. We broke off the upper stalks of the youngest plants and immediately found ourselves in the stalking business again. The lower, older stems are hollow and woody, but the upper six inches of newly grown stem was solid, tender, and easily peeled, leaving only the green heart of the stalk and tiny, yellowish, unfolding leaves at the terminal end. With the bitter cortex gone and the milky sap washed away, these were mild enough to include in a salad. Of course David loved them. Boiled only about two minutes, then buttered, they were delicious. Cooked by my bacon recipe they were superb.

I have often admired the beautiful pink or white flowers of the musk mallow (*Malva moschata*) as I drove through New York and New England or even southeastern Canada. Although I know that all species of *Malva* are more or less edible, and none poisonous, I had never experimented with this plant for food, as it doesn't grow around my area of Pennsylvania. The plants reach one to two feet high, and the flowers resemble small hollyhocks or hibiscus blossoms, about two inches across. The leaves of those around Ithaca are dissected into five lobes, which are further dissected into more lobes bearing still other lobes, giving the entire rounded leaf a lacy effect. The flowers are followed by calyx-covered, wheel-like fruits resembling undersized hollyhock buttons. These with the calyx peeled away are eaten by children and are called "Doll's cheeses."

These little cheeses, only about a half-inch in diameter, are so mild in flavor that some of our nature walkers thought them tasteless. But boiled for about thirty minutes until tender—green calyces and all—then seasoned with salt and butter, they were very good, still slightly crunchy, with a mucilaginous texture that made them slide down easily. Musk mallow is a quite passable food that I suspect is quite nourishing, though its food value has never been explored.

Besides these new discoveries, old plant friends were abundant in the area. We ate the last of the wild strawberries and the first of the wild mazzard cherries on the same day. Cattails were in just the right stage so I could demonstrate the five different foods this plant furnishes: the green bloom spike for boiling and buttering; the cossack asparagus that is the peeled, white base of the stalk eaten either raw or cooked; the pollen from blooms too old to eat that can be mixed with flour to make some very palatable golden flapjacks; the ropy rhizomes with their starchy cores that can be roasted around a fire and eaten, or dried and made into a fine white flour that makes excellent bread. The white sprouts at the end of the rhizomes, which will be next year's cattails, can be broken off and boiled as a hearty, starchy vegetable. Pigweed or lamb's-quarters (*Chenopodium album*) was at the right stage to be cooked like spinach. Huge, tender thistle stalks (*Cirsium vulgare*) had just shot up in preparation for blooming. Armed with unlimited enthusiasm and heavy gloves, we peeled these stems, sliced them crosswise,

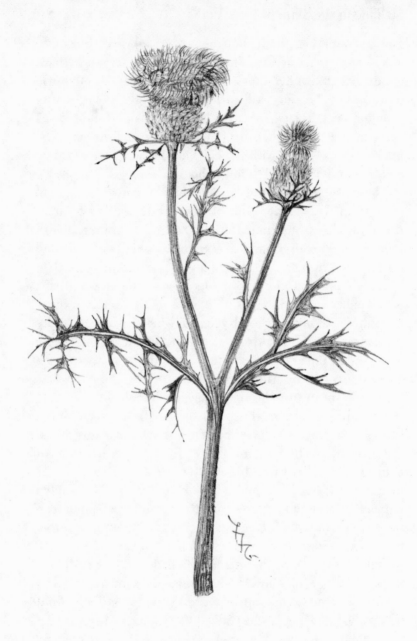

common thistle

(*Cirsium vulgare*)

and boiled them to create a vegetable dish that resembles artichoke hearts in flavor. Great burdock (*Arctium lappa*) was putting up massive bloom stalks that could be peeled, sliced, and cooked into a filling, nutritious vegetable dish. There were several dozen other interesting wild vegetables in our walking area which were explained, sampled, admired, and wondered at.

The walks lasted about two hours each, and at the end of each one we found David with a sampling of cooked wild delicacies to distribute among the people who had just been turned on to this kind of food. I hope those who shared these wild walks enjoyed them as much as I did.

10. Gathering of the Wild Gourmets

O N THE third weekend of September, wild food freaks from many states converge on North Bend State Park, near Cairo, West Virginia, to display their own special culinary creations and to sample those of others. They call it Nature Wonder Weekend. When this annual affair was first dreamed up, the sponsors wondered if there was enough interest in nature's wild foods to attract anyone besides me. The number who attend—limited by the park's facilities to about 125—has been reached every year, and last year more than twice that many were turned away.

People come to teach, brag, learn, and share fellowship with kindred souls. There simply is no better short course on the wonderful things that can be done with the free, naturally grown health foods that nature so graciously offers to those who know how to find them. And it is being held in the right place. There are a few places in the world that have more wild food per acre than Appalachia and the valleys of the streams that run into the Ohio River. In West Virginia one can find such arctic survivals as crowberries, creeping snowberries, bunchberries, and two kinds of cranberries in the cold mountain bogs, while—only a few miles away—grow such Southerners as persimmons, pawpaws, muscadines, and water chinquapins.

The first event was a social hour (which lasted two and a half hours) where wild beverages and wild hors d'oeuvres were served. This was held in a spacious patio surrounded by tasteful displays of the wild food plants found in West Virginia. Each guest, upon arriving, was handed a tag with the name of a food plant on it, then told to find the plant in the display and attach this label to it. Mild cheating was condoned, so the labels eventually found their ways to the right plants.

The nibbles were wonderful and far too numerous to list. I was especially impressed by the dilled purslane stems, the persimmon muffins, the pawpaw cookies, and some forty other wild-food tidbits. There was a demonstration on the easy ways to crack wild black walnuts, hickory nuts, and hazelnuts, and plenty of these to practice on. Provided for the lazy were dishes of these nuts already shelled and salted. Beverages ranged from wild teas of many kinds through wild fruit punches to some elderberry and wild grape wines.

We went almost directly from this feast to a sumptuous dinner prepared by the park chef. This meal was founded on rare roast beef and baked potatoes, but even the chef got into the act by serving pickled poke stems and elderberry cobbler. The social hour hadn't noticeably dulled any appetites, and we did justice to a very good dinner.

We all adjourned to a small auditorium for lectures, slide and film shows, and the question-answer period—all on wild foods. To reassure people from far places that wild food gathering wasn't strictly a West Virginia sport, I showed slides and gave a talk on wild food gathering in such far-flung

places as Arizona and Maine. I showed them how to peel a
prickly pear and roast agave hearts in underground ovens as
the Indians did it, as well as how to remove the roe from
green sea urchins, how to clean the seeds from a Maine wild
rose hip and stuff the cavity with wild red raspberries, plus
many other tricks of this non-trade.

There were still two big surprises to come that evening. An
adult education class in wild food cookery—given by the
Parkersburg, West Virginia, school system—had made up
great quantities of wild fruit jams and jellies, and had
gathered and dried many kinds of wild teas. These they had
packed into gift boxes, four half-pint jars to the box, to give
to everyone attending, besides a few gatecrashers. They were
given with the admonition to "go and do likewise"—that is,
each recipient was encouraged to eat the contents of these
jars, then refill them with their own creations as a gift to
someone else who might appreciate delicacies from nature's
bounty. Don't be surprised if you receive a wild Christmas
package!

After the gift-giving, another wild smorgasbord was
wheeled in. The *pièce de résistance* was a great haunch of
roast venison, but this was preceded by a real gourmet sour
sorrel soup. There were side dishes of milkweed buds in
hollandaise sauce and a salad based on wild watercress, but
also containing oxalis, lamb's-quarters, purslane, and a hint
of wild garlic. There were more wild teas and fruit punches—
and finally, there was dandelion root coffee and black walnut
cake baked by last year's first-prize winner of the Black
Walnut Festival baking contest.

They couldn't seem to quit. One enthusiast set up a camp
stove on the table and prepared fried water chinquapins, nuts
about the size of a small acorn produced by some oversized
water-lilies that inhabit sluggish backwaters of the local
streams and ponds. They have a flavor like mixed nuts and
popcorn. They went fast. For the extremely daring, he

prepared some fried blacksnake fillets and some fried grass-hoppers. The grasshoppers were surprisingly good, having a crisp texture and a nutty flavor with a hint of the taste of shrimp. The snake meat tasted like a cross between chicken and fish.

I am pleased to report that, despite all the massive eating of strange foods, no one became ill. Everybody was back for more by breakfast time. Breakfast wasn't wild, but it did have a Southern twang: fried apples, grits, homemade sausage patties, and scrambled eggs.

It was a beautiful fall day after a showery night, and the whole group set off on a field trip. They soon learned to find the wild food plants growing in their native habitats, and we were able to examine over sixty plants on this two-hour walk. We found some areas where whole families could live well for months on wild food alone. But even manna from heaven would pall if one had to eat nothing else for any length of time. Wild foods, to continue to be attractive, must come in fifty-seven varieties—and in West Virginia, in its usual hospitable way, furnishes several times this number for those who know nature's food secrets.

The walk ended at a picnic area where we were met by a truck from the park lodge carrying tasty box lunches that we supplemented with wild delicacies gathered along the way. There was a final question period for those who found they needed more information. New friendships were made, invitations extended, addresses exchanged, and plans for future get-togethers made. Then we broke up, with happy memories of a wonderful weekend where Mother Nature had presided as chief entertainer and hostess.

11. Going Wild in San Francisco

IT WAS October. The host on an early morning TV show was interviewing me. I had landed at the San Francisco International Airport at 10 P.M. the evening before. This interviewer was interested in the availability of wild foods in the Bay Area. I told him that I had already found three edible wild plants growing as weeds in the flower beds that surrounded the TV studios as I came in, but had to confess that I didn't know a nearby place where I could gather wild foods in quantity. I have probably spent a total of five days in that beautiful city, always as a one-day visitor, and my favorite survival spot was the restaurants on Fisherman's Wharf. However, from the brief glimpse of the flora I had on my way to the station, I was willing to bet that I could find enough wild food for a good vegetarian lunch, and do it before lunchtime.

He called my bluff, and offered to send a camera crew along with me to record the gathering. I wanted neither a well-groomed park nor a dense forest. The camera crew

thought we could find a neglected area in a park they knew
and we set off. We never got there. As we passed through an
urban-renewal area where slum buildings were coming down
and jackhammers machinegunned their way through concrete, I spotted a block-long median strip in the wide street
that had been allowed to grow completely wild.

. This was in the well-watered fog belt and the growth was
lush. The strip had been planted in young olive trees several
years before, and these were about eight feet tall and
beginning to bear. But olive foliage is so thin that it scarcely
interfered with the sunlight that filtered through, and wild
food plants grew bountiful right up to the bases of the little
trees. Before I had even stepped into this natural greengro-
cery I had spotted eight different wild food plants, and all of
them in great abundance.

There were tall lamb's-quarters (*Chenopodium*) and wild
beets (*Amaranthus*), both relatives of common garden spinach and furnishing the same kind of vegetable. Wild mustard
(*Brassica*), charlock (*Raphanus*), and, as a complete surprise
to me, orach (*Atriplex*), which I had seen only by the seaside
or growing in saline desert soils. These three could furnish
more green vegetables or salads, and the buds of the two
members of the mustard family could be cooked and served
like broccoli. There was a fat-rooted, biennial thistle (*Cirsium*), and the tender, crisp root had the flavor of a globe
artichoke. Between the taller plants, purslane (*Portulaca*)
sprawled over the ground, offering crisp, purple stems and
leafy tips. Both are very good, raw or cooked. Then there
were, of course, dandelions, in every stage of development,
offering dandelion greens, crowns, and roots, all good cooked
vegetables, and the tender hearts are delicious in salads.

By this time the camera crew was ready to concede that I
could not only prepare a lunch from the available wild food
here, but could easily vegetable-feed a large family indefinitely from this natural wild food supermarket. We started

filming the gathering and immediately attracted a crowd.
Although it was during school hours, two little black boys
about ten years old attached themselves to us. One was a shy
lad wearing a sombrero almost as wide as he was tall. The
other was bold, beautiful, and intelligent. He amazed me by
joining in the eating of raw purslane and orach, saying that
he often came out here and finished up his dinner when the
food was scanty at home. He led me through the rank growth
to his favotite patch of what he called "wild lemon grass"
(*Oxalis*) and we added this acid, lemon-flavored plant with
cloverlike leaves to our snack. Then he spotted a tall plant
with lacy, dark-green foliage with umbels of yellowish flowers
and maturing seed-heads at its top. He grew excited and
pointed, "Hey, I know what that plant is, that's lickwish." It
was a wild anise plant, but many think anise and licorice taste
almost identical. He started pulling the blooms and immature seeds of the umbels and cramming them into his mouth,
saying around a mouthful of anise, "Man, just taste that
sweetness. Sometimes I call this lickwish and sometimes I
just call it sugar." A thrill shot through me to find a modern
boy who knew how to get his sweets from the wild. He had
thought it all through about sanitation also, for he later said,
"This lickwish out here is clean, cause no dogs ever come out
here. When it grows close to the sidewalk you ought not to
eat it because it might have dog wee-wee on it."

Then I found a clump of wild lettuce (*Lactuca*) with
plants in all stages of development, from just peeping
through the ground to seeding. The California climate is
wonderful, but it is apparently confusing to plants trying to
figure out when spring has come. It is just about spring all
year. There had recently been an abundance of rain and
everything was growing enthusiastically, with a whole crop of
new plants coming up. I was able to gather very young wild
lettuce, which is good for cooking like spinach, one of the
most palatable of all wild greens, and also to gather tender

stems from older plants that, when peeled, make a very good cooked vegetable.

We also located a nice patch of sheep sorrel. This would make a good addition to a purslane salad, can form the main ingredient in a gourmet soup and can even be cooked with sugar to make a fruitlike dessert. The olive trees, while not exactly wild, would come within my rules of fair foraging, which is "reaping where you did not sow, but only if the food would go unused unless you take it." They were just beginning to bear, but in the block-long median strip with its two rows of young olive trees, there were many bushels of olives just turning from green to bluish-black. An olive is inedible straight from the tree. To prepare them for eating is a long, complicated pickling process, but the nearly ripe olives would be just right for making olive oil. Strangely enough, making olive oil is a simpler process than making the olives edible. Slightly underripe olives merely need the seeds removed, then the meat is pressed. It is better to put them in a cloth bag, place the bag between two boards and load the top board with heavy stones. This gently squeezes out the "virgin" oil, the very finest of olive oils.

I was beginning to wish that I had brought along my camping gear and back-pack tent. I would have loved to set up my tent right there in the midst of the noisy city, gathered and cooked my food from the wild for a day or so, and proved that nature can do her thing wherever man will let a small plot of fertile soil alone.

I would still like to return and try that stunt with my two oldest grandchildren, Mike and Colleen, who like wild food as well as I do. But I doubt that it will be possible in exactly the same place. The film the crew made was shown on television the next day, and within two hours the median strip was covered with curious people who came to see what had been there all the time. They had been unable to see it until their eyes had been opened.

12. Sea and Desert—
Land of Wild
Food Aplenty

WE WERE returning from Tiburon Island in the Sea of Cortez—known to most Americans as the Gulf of California—in a stiffened inflatable raft invented by Jacques-Yves Cousteau, the famous diver. It's supposed to be the safest seagoing, portable, inflatable vessel afloat—we needed these qualities, for the hard spring winds were whipping up a steep channel sea that would endanger a less able boat. Safe that boat might have been, but comfortable in that sea it was not.

We sighted one of these less able boats wallowing through the heavy seas toward us. It was a Seri Indian boat, planked on hand-hewn frames, but driven—incongruously—by a modern outboard motor. The helmsman, a fierce-looking old Seri, was wrapped in a piece of black plastic as protection from the waves hitting him and streaming down into the boat. The caves of Tiburon Island were once the home of the Seri Indians. These people were formerly cannibals, and not so "formerly" as you might think. Only a few years ago the Mexican Government forcibly moved them to the mainland where they could be more easily controlled, as too many Mexican fishermen were disappearing in the neighborhood of Tiburon Island. We could make out four other water-soaked people on the Seri boat, two of them bailing madly to keep it afloat. As the boat approached, I saw that the four passengers were my son-in-law and my three grandchildren.

My daughter and I had been with an expedition of students, teaching them how to use the wild foods of this sea and its adjacent desert land. Her husband had unexpectedly received a few days off from his job, so he and the children decided to join us for a few days of wild camping in Mexico after our expedition was over. Since we had just spent two weeks on a desert island, we wanted to sample some new kind of habitat. We held a bouncing conference on the waves, and decided to sail to a lagoon area on the mainland for a new adventure. We transferred two of the children to our raft to lighten their frail boat and headed for the mainland.

What the Mexicans call a *laguna* in this part of Mexico is really a saltwater tidal creek that sometimes reaches lagoon proportions at high tide. It is a surprising thing to come on one of these on this arid coast—the Sonoran Desert—where you see only the gray-green of desert vegetation until you come over a hill and see miles of bright-green mangroves winding over desert flats, with glints of bright water that runs with the tides inland for six hours and then seaward for the next six.

We pitched our camp on the lagoon shores and assembled our folding kayak. My son-in-law, grandson, and I discriminated against the women by taking the first kayak voyage down the lagoon. From the water you would never guess the creek flowed through a desert, for it was almost completely screened with mangroves. The mangrove is an interesting tree, except that here you can never tell where one tree starts and another stops, for they all seem to be connected, forming impenetrable thickets with few openings. Each trunk that holds up the continuous, interconnected top is surrounded by dozens of prop-roots, which come out of the saltwater from all angles to join the trunk at different levels. We marveled at its unique means of reproduction—the seeds sprout while still clinging to the parent tree and form slender seedlings which resemble sharp-pointed cigars. By some miracle of nature these drop only at low tide, and the sharp end penetrates the mud, holding fast until it can put out its rootlets.

As the tide was lowering, some islands appeared above the surface. We landed on one of these, where we dug clams with our bare hands. Soon we had enough for a huge chowder. These luscious butter clams, *Saxidomus nuttali*, were already familiar to me, as I had dug them years ago on the coast of California.

Further down, near the sea, we found great, green beds of a tender annual species of *Salicornia*, or glasswort, looking like green lawns on the higher tide flats. The young plants make an excellent salad or cooked vegetable that is naturally salted with mineral-rich sea salt. Nearby grew seaside purslane, a ground-hugging, sprawling plant with fleshy, edible leaves. These two plants can provide much-needed green vegetables for dwellers on arid coasts. When wild stands become insufficient, they can be raised in gardens irrigated with saltwater.

We gathered a supply of each and, when the tide turned, paddled back to our camp. We soon had a geographically misplaced but still delicious New England clam chowder bubbling on the camp fire! The seaside purslane was made into a fresh salad and the glasswort was boiled (only a few minutes' cooking makes it perfectly tender), then cooled and covered with salad dressing. It was a rare treat. Both these plants must have ample vitamin C, since they were called "scurvy grass" by ancient sailors. I would judge by their strong green color alone that both are rich in vitamin A. I'm sure they absorb tremendous amounts of essential minerals from the seawater on which they survive.

After our excellent dinner, we armed ourselves with nets and flashlights and set out to stalk the wily crab of this coast. This time we didn't take the kayak, but merely waded in the shallow lagoon and spotted the crabs by shining the flashlights through the clear water to the sandy bottom. These crabs, called Gulf Blues, are huge, containing more delicious crabmeat than any crab I have ever eaten—and I have eaten a great many kinds. They certainly deserve their Latin name, *Callinectes bellicosus*, for a more belligerent crab does not exist. They are swimming crabs, with the hindmost feet modified into a pair of efficient oars, and are closely related to the Eastern blue crab found along the Atlantic Coast and in Chesapeake Bay—although they are a little larger, slightly longer in body, and a more intense and electric blue than their Eastern cousins.

When first spotted in the beam of a flashlight they usually attempt to swim or scuttle sideways out of the light. They never run far, for they would rather fight than run. When cornered, they throw up their fierce claws, and offer to do battle with all comers. Then they can be netted and dropped into a bag. It sounds easy, but I think every one of us made a small blood donation trying to get the crabs to turn loose and drop into the bag. We shortly had all the crabs we could hope to use.

We boiled them as soon as we returned to camp, then started a second dinner. After we had all we could eat, we still picked out about a pound of crab meat that we scrambled with eggs for breakfast the next morning.

On that second day we really hit the jackpot in the seafood line. First my daughter and son-in-law paddled out to an offshore shallow where an Indian had told us we could find "Chinese scallops." With snorkel gear they soon collected a boatload and brought them in. I had no idea what kind of creature this Indian was calling Chinese scallop, and was agreeably surprised to find it was my old friend from Florida, the *Pinna*, or pen shell, not even closely related to the true scallop—but eaten like a scallop and even tastier. We cut out the oversized adductor muscles and had a scallop fry right on the beach.

My daughter and son-in-law had become enamored with skin-diving, so we let them return to the scallop beds, while the children and I walked around the shore to a rocky headland in hopes of finding some life-filled tidepools. We found many such pools, some of them in beach caves, which the blue water colored a deep azure with its reflection. They were fantastically beautiful. The deep pools were alive with fish, but I had brought along only a fish spear, which was useless in these deep pools. The children excitedly gathered the beautiful seashells that are cast up at every tide, while I got together a bagful of sea urchins—whose roe is more delicious than caviar.

Then we came on a shallow, rocky tidepool and I saw a huge spiny lobster, *Panulirus interruptus*, with the upward bend of his blue-striped legs actually out of the water. I approached this giant from the seaward side of the pool—my heart pounding. Finally I made a grab, caught him at the base of his huge antennae, and lifted him ashore. The children danced about in ecstatic excitement. Then Mike, my grandson, spotted another lobster partly hidden under a rock—only about half as large as the first one, but still good-sized—which soon joined the other in our game-bag.

A little further on we came to where the incoming tide was

just beginning to break through a hole in the rocks into a large tidepool. Clustered about this hole were many many three- and four-pound fish apparently trying to get into the filling pool. They were skittish, but after I sat quietly with my spear in the water, one swam under it. I lunged down and got him. We got two more and were extremely proud of the food we were contributing to the family table.

Walking homeward, one of the girls spotted an octopus in a very small tidepool. He quickly slipped under a stone and, while I could reach in and feel him, I couldn't pull him loose from his anchorage. The children had seen too many TV shows, depicting the harmless octopus as a dangerous creature, to risk putting their hands under the stone, but they did volunteer to help me turn it over. With all four of us straining our utmost, we finally did turn it over and that silly octopus crawled right out of the pool onto the bank to join our other foodstuffs. I had learned to eat octopus in Hawaii, and knew it to be delicious when properly prepared.

Three prouder children—and, for that matter, a prouder grandpa—you never saw.

Food was now in such abundance that we had to cease gathering, giving us time to explore the desert that lay outside the mangroves. The only edible wild food we found were ocotilla blossoms, which are good either as a vegetable or cooked with honey or raw sugar. However, I was able to point out five kinds of cactus that would bear delicious fruit later in the year.

The only way we could get the children to agree to terminate this trip was to promise them we would return at another season and sample still more of the delicacies this wonderful land offers to those who know how to take and use her gifts.

13. A Love Affair
South of the Border

I'VE FOUND a new love. It's the Sea of Cortez in Mexico—usually marked on maps of the United States as the Gulf of California. I love it with the same passion I feel for the islands off the coast of Maine, for the rolling countryside of central Pennsylvania, for the mountains of West Virginia, and for the Quetico-Superior canoe wilderness of northern Minnesota, and southwestern Ontario.

But there will be no jealousy in this love affair! I am getting to be an old man—and, appropriately, the mistress I really love is a mature woman. She is faithful and devoted. Whenever I travel, she is there before me, to greet me as I arrive. She is old Mother Nature herself.

I am a seeker of wild and remote places, but I am not a loner. Part of the joy of exploring new places is sharing with a knowledgeable companion the happiness I find in nature. I asked another man's wife to accompany me to the Sea of Cortez. She's my son-in-law's wife, my daughter, Pat. They live in Tucson, Arizona, and are the parents of three of my favorite grandchildren.

We left Tucson late in the afternoon, and by the time we had completed the formalities at the border in Nogales it was dark. We drove into a strange land and into the night. The road south was excellent. Two coyotes crossed ahead of us, and our lights picked out the eyes of numerous small animals along the roadside. By bedtime we reached the city of Hermosilla ("the beautiful little one") and rented rooms in a luxurious motel at what seemed to us a trifling price.

At sunup Pat pounded on my door and told me to come quickly. I threw on some clothes and rushed out prepared to defend her against hordes of Mexican bandits. She only wanted me to see the glorious sunrise and start identifying all the exotic tropical plants she had found in the motel garden and grounds. She had been out among them since daylight. This was even more nature-enthusiasm than I usually demand in a companion. There were bananas, date palms, guavas, loquats, strange cacti, hibiscus, birds-of-paradise, and many other warm-country plants that were strange to her.

We drove on to Guaymas, about midway down the eastern shore of the Sea of Cortez. Here we watched ancient, work-worn shrimp boats unloading their catch, sampled the local seafoods cooked in the Mexican manner, and explored the parks and gardens about the old city. But the Guaymas Harbor was a very unsatisfactory part of the sea we had come to see, so we moved up to San Carlos Bay. We rented an outboard motorboat and then set out to find some shores that had not been ruined by man. We were told the sea was rough outside the bay, but to one used to the Atlantic off Maine shores it seemed a flat calm. There were only a few smooth oily swells. We headed for a shore that looked fairly close in this crystal-clear air. It took two hours of not-at-all-unpleasant boating to get there.

Here was the kind of terrain we were seeking. We entered

a tidal creek, and even before we landed I saw great patches of the glasswort (*Salicornia*) that is related to our domestic beets and Swiss chard, and is a very good raw vegetable, cooked or pickled. This plant can live where it is covered by high tides, and can use sea water as moisture. We also saw large mats of sea purslane (*Trianthema portulacastrum*) with succulent, fleshy leaves and tender stems. Making an impromptu salad on the spot, we found these tasty plants delightfully salted with the sea salt they take up in their juices. I made a mental note to bring apple cider vinegar on the expedition, for both these plants are delicious when a little acid is added.

Pat crossed the low dunes to the outer beach and started collecting shells, which were in such profusion and beauty that one suspected it had been a long time since a shell collector had visited here. I first walked up the tidal creek until it spread out into a mangrove swamp. I love these strange trees with aerial prop-roots to which tiny oysters cling, and their amazing seeds that sprout on the trees, grow into little spears, and then fall only when the tide is out. The tide was approaching low now, so I walked downstream to where the creek spread out into a sandy flat before joining the sea. Here numerous little squirts betrayed the presence of clams and cockles. They were so shallow and the sand was so easily dug that one didn't need a shovel or clam fork. With bare hands I turned up a dozen good-sized butter clams in a minute or two, and could have filled the boat had I any use for so many.

These were very similar to the butter clams I had learned to love in the state of Washington, years ago, and there are few better clams. This is the *Saxidomus nuttali* and I had also met him before in Southern California. The cockles were even easier to get, often lying half-exposed. These would make wonderful chowder for the expedition.

When Pat came back triumphantly carrying two shopping bags full of exquisite shells, we pushed the boat away and went to a cliff-bound shore that beckoned. Carefully conning the boat into a little inlet, we found a beautiful little private beach, all our own, inaccessible from either side. Here were so many more beautiful shells that Pat dumped her shopping bags into the bottom of the boat and started reloading them from the new supply. At the level the tide would be when high, now many feet above the water, was a ledge on which we could walk around the cave-filled cliff. Every sea cave at high tide level was a treasure trove of new shells, and Pat was ecstatic. Around a bend the ledge widened out and became a solid-rock flat, dotted with tide pools from the size of a wash basin to the size of an Olympic pool.

The water in these pools was so crystal clear that one could see every detail. Sea anemones flowered from the rock walls; strange, huge, many-armed starfish clung over shellfish, patiently exerting pressure until they finally wore them down and opened them, then nastily digested the shells' contents by actually inverting their stomachs into the shells. Purple sea urchins crowded every crack in the walls and bottoms of the pools, a promise of some good eating for the expedition, since sea-urchin roe is as delicious and delicate as the finest caviar.

I opened the clams I had dug, and threw the contents into the tide pool. Fish darted out from dozens of unsuspected hiding places and quickly gobbled up this treat. One such tide pool could furnish more fish than any family could eat. Any crumbs that escaped the fish and settled to the bottom were promptly taken by half a dozen huge spiny lobsters that appeared from seemingly nowhere. Life, life, teeming life, on what many would see only as a barren, sterile shore!

On the way back to the bay we went ashore again, where the beach was narrow and the upper shore steep. When we climbed to the top of the shore we were suddenly in the Sonoran Desert. But it is desert only because life has deserted it. Here the plants have learned to conserve the little water that falls, go dormant in dry weather, and then in a spring rain burst into riotous bloom, which is followed by fruit. Yuccas will produce edible bloom stalks next spring; the century plant signaling from distant hills could furnish huge amounts of good food right now, and when that long-delayed bloom stalk starts up it can furnish both food and drink.

Then there are the forests of cacti. The sweet pitahaya and the sour pitahaya will both bear beautiful blooms followed by delicious fruit. The prickly pear, locally called *"tuna"* is almost a staff of life, furnishing fruit and a good vegetable. The mighty saguaros have a fine fruit, if you fasten a small blade to the longest bamboo pole you can find to cut it down. Some of the barrel cacti have excellent fruit. The succulent flesh inside that tough barrel is mostly water and has saved many a desert traveler's life. The Indians once hollowed out the tops of these barrels, and used them for cooking pots, boiling their food in them by dropping hot stones into the liquid. Even the organ-pipe cactus has delicious fruit for those who know how to gather and disarm it.

Nature will not only help those who know and trust her to survive, even in a desert, but, if one loves her enough to get to really know her, she will shower them with luxuries.

On the way back to the boat docks we stopped and swapped a few lies with the fishermen whose boats were crowding into one area where the fish were biting well. They were pulling in ruby snappers from one to two feet long. These are not considered a particularly exciting game fish, but they are a beautiful clear red on the back, shading into rose then pink on the sides, with a white belly. The fishermen told us they were the finest eating in the Sea of Cortez. We

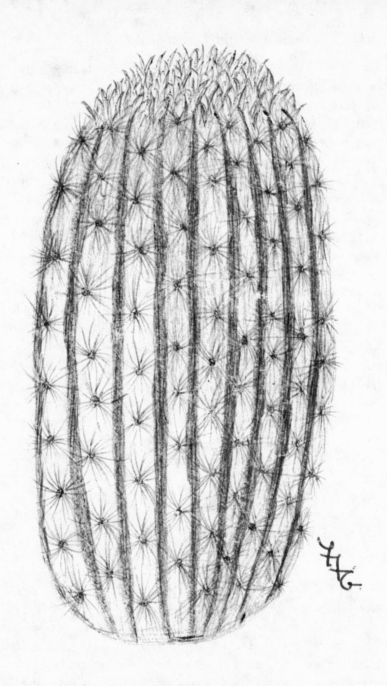

barrel cactus

(*Echinocactus franklinii*)

were not cooking our own meals on this trip, so we were not tempted to fish or take any of the other delicious seafoods we found. We returned our boat then, with sea-stimulated appetites, went to the nearest restaurant and ordered ruby snapper for dinner. It was superb!

II. Some Thoughts
on the
Right Way
to Live

14. Which Generation Gap?

SOMETIMES, when I read my voluminous mail, I get the impression that a great many people consider me about the only possible source of information on wild foods. Let me hasten to assure you that I am in no way unique. There are many experts on wild food plants, and more are being built all the time. You'd be surprised how often I learn something new from my readers. It happens nearly every day.

I have a friend—which is not too surprising, for even weed-eaters can make and retain a few friends, if they go a bit easy on that wild garlic. Nor is it too surprising that this special friend is a naturalist, and an excellent one. He is also a wild food eater, and I doubt that I could teach him much about the wild foods that grow anywhere in the northeastern quarter of our country. A skilled fisherman and seafood gatherer, he will usually find some high-protein foods to go with his wild fruits, vegetables, and nuts. He is an epicure with very sensitive and highly trained tastebuds and one of the best camp cooks that I know. He is constantly inventing new and better ways to make wild foods into delicacies.

One would expect that I would seek out such a person as my best friend. We often love people mainly because they love the things we love, and Mark and I have shared many joys in many places together while indulging our mutual love of nature and what she can offer us. The only surprising thing about this friendship is that Mark is eighteen now and I am sixty. Even more unusual, Mark and I have been on this best-friend basis for more than ten years. We first met on Mark's eighth birthday, appropriately enough, in a rich, stream-bottom wood in Pennsylvania. I was gathering wild leeks, or "ramps" as they are known by those who love them best, and Mark was gathering wild chervil. We immediately pooled our efforts and began filling our baskets and plastic bags with wild edibles.

In a marshy spot we found a bed of wild watercress and nearby were cattails just beginning to show. These are tedious at that time of year, but we had all the time there was and we peeled a bagful of the tender sprouts, which have a delicious flavor like cucumber. The calamus sprouts were even more tedious, for one gets an inch-long heart about a quarter-inch in diameter, but they have so much flavor one wants very few in a salad. Near the calamus swamp some whitish, last-year's stems, fine as sewing thread, betrayed the presence of groundnuts, or Indian potatoes. These were so near the surface that we could pull up whole strings of them without even digging in the soft, recently thawed ground. Near the top of the ridge we found wintergreen berries, much fatter and juicier than they had been the previous fall. Then, as we walked across an old orchard, we came upon the greatest treasure of the day, enough morels—or "sponge mushrooms" as Mark called them—to fill several plastic bags.

When I remarked that wandering alone in the woods seemed a strange way for an eight-year-old to be celebrating

wild leek or ramp
(*Allium tricoccum*)

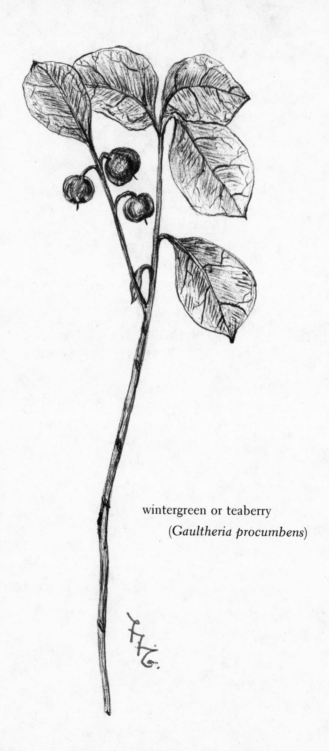

wintergreen or teaberry
(*Gaultheria procumbens*)

his birthday, Mark tossed his tow-colored hair out of his blue eyes and said, "I'd rather be out here gathering wild food than watching the best movie Hollywood ever made." Of course that won my heart. At that time Mark was still trying to convert his family to wild-food eating, and as a special treat his mother had agreed to cook any wild foods he could find for his birthday party. I followed him home, met his charming parents, brothers and sisters, and hinted so broadly that they almost had to invite me, as the only outsider, to the birthday party.

When Mark's mother had made her rash promise she had expected no more than a little wild chervil to add to the salad. But when she found that we intended to have fried groundnuts; ramps in cheese sauce; morels sautéed in butter; a complete salad of watercress, cattail, and calamus hearts; wintergreen berries and wild chervil; plus a wintergreen tea made from some of the plants we had gathered, she turned most of the cooking over to us. She prepared the fried chicken and the birthday cake.

Thus began a relationship that still continues, and it has enriched both of our lives. Every year Mark and I spend some time together in intimate communion with nature, absorbing the many things she still has to teach both of us. We have gone on a number of survival trips together, subsisting for up to a week entirely on wild foods. We have never gone hungry. Such outings have always become continuous feasts.

The first such survival trip that we shared was when Mark was only nine. We chose an island in a shallow bay in Maine. It didn't prove too wise a choice, for when the mighty tides of Maine went out we were surrounded by vast, gooey, smelly, mudflats. By slogging through the mud for half-a-mile toward the mouth of the bay, we could reach some excellent clam beds and mussel clusters. The little island furnished plenty of wild berries and red wild raspberries, and an unlimited supply of seaside wild vegetables such as orach or seaside spinach, glasswort, sea blite, and the hot, horseradish-like sea rocket to add zip to our cuisine.

The first day we breakfasted on such vegetarian fare. Then, as the tide was getting low, we set off across the mudflat to get some more substantial food. Going out was not too bad, as we were fresh, well-fed, and carrying no more than a clam fork and some containers in which to bring home the loot. We found not only clams and mussels; but around the scattered boulders that dotted the outer beach we discovered many periwinkles or seasnails, a delicious seafood; and at the water's edge at low tide there were unlimited numbers of sea urchins that were well filled with orange-yellow roe or eggs, which are very nutritious.

I didn't relish the idea of crossing the sticky mudflat every time I was hungry, so decided to take back a large supply of all these delectable creatures and dig a little saltwater pool at our island's edge where I could keep them fresh and eminently available. As I am prone to do with most things pertaining to wild food, I overdid it. We must have collected more than a hundred pounds of heavy shelly seafoods.

Mark was game to put a large portion of them in his knapsack, but my own load must have weighed close to seventy-five pounds. Our loads made us sink lower into sticky mud. It was real work to get our feet free from the muck in order to take another step. It took more than an hour to cross the stretch of mud. We kept silent since all the energy we could gather had to be put into the effort to get back to solid ground.

By this time the tide was rolling back in. It seemed to be gaining on us. There was no danger, as the water would be little over knee-deep at high tide, but the waves lapping at our feet spurred us on. With only a hundred yards to go we stopped for a last rest. Mark said, "I didn't know a survival trip was going to be like this." I felt guilty about subjecting the little fellow to this kind of torture, and tried to cheer him up by pointing out that solid ground was only a few more minutes away. He turned a surprised look my way and said, "Oh, I'm not kicking; I just meant that I didn't know it would be so wonderful and thrilling." Who could help loving such a spirit?

He has kept that same spirit, and now, as he approaches his nineteenth year, this spirit—his unbounded enthusiasm and his eager curiosity—has brought him a greater knowledge of nature's best secrets than many naturalists acquire in a lifetime. We have had many wonderful outings together (and he has led groups of his own), have made films together for television shows, and I'm sure I have profited as much from the relationship as Mark has.

One time a reporter covering one of our wild food trips asked Mark if he thought of me as a father or a teacher. With no hesitation whatever Mark answered, "Neither. He is my friend."

15. How Organic Farming Can Save Our Air

WITH all the sudden concern about pollution and the deterioration of the environment, organic gardeners and farmers have been abruptly elevated to a new status. Now everyone is anxious about the poisons in our food, our air, our streams, and our soil. Multitudes are preaching that man's relationship with nature should be one of cooperation rather than brutal conquest, and that we must conserve and reuse our waste materials. It's high time for the organic enthusiast to step forward and modestly proclaim that this is what he has been talking about all along. The organic gardener has been a sort of literary joke, considered by the "economic man" as a kook, a crank, a crackpot, or a cultist. But now the public is grinning out of the other side of its mouth, and millions are ready to concede that the organic people have been right.

The organic person has the answers in more ways than one. Since this great furor on lowering the quality of the environment began, I have attended many meetings of those concerned about doing something to reverse our present disastrous trend. One striking thing about these gatherings is the number of people who moan about the cost of conservation and the things we must give up in order to live nonpolluting lives. Any man who has left the noise, foul air, chlorinated and fluoridated water, littered streets, and the filth and dirt of a large city to live on an organic homestead knows that the gains of more natural living far outweigh the things one must give up to practice it. Nothing could be more expensive than our present wasteful, throwaway culture that is reducing the value of our environment at an astronomical rate. Because of inexorable natural laws, man must make choices—this is nothing new. Often these choices are not between good and bad, but between two goods, and then man must decide which one has the greater value. This makes the choices of improving and preserving a livable environment pretty easy.

Man must choose between the convenience of non-returnable bottles and living on the dump, for our non-returnable, nondisposable containers will rapidly make the whole earth into nothing but a junkheap. We must choose between reusing our sewage and garbage as valuable plant food, or having all our streams polluted. Very shortly we may have to choose whether we will run our automobiles in the cities or breathe air so foul that it can kill. And some day we may have to decide whether we will use available oxygen to run engines or to breathe.

To understand what organic gardeners have to do with the available oxygen in our atmosphere, we need a little background on what modern scientists are thinking. There seems to be plenty of evidence that all—or at least nearly all—of the free oxygen in our atmosphere is of organic origin; that is, it was released as a by-product of photosynthesis, the process by which the green chlorophyll cells in plants, using light for power, break down carbon dioxide, make food for the plant from the carbon, and release the oxygen as refuse. Back in the Carboniferous Period it is thought that the atmosphere contained a great deal more carbon dioxide than it now does, and the carbon dioxide was lessened and the oxygen increased by the rampant growth of the Coal Age plants that were peculiarly adapted to this kind of atmosphere.

Since all green plants still consume the carbon of carbon dioxide and still release the free oxygen, it would seem that all we have to do to have our oxygen replenished is keep plenty of green plants growing—but there is a catch to it. When the plant material decays or is burned, the carbon again combines with the oxygen and turns back into carbon dioxide. Each plant, whether it be a microscopic cell of alga or a giant redwood tree, produces only enough oxygen in its lifetime to recombine with the carbon in its cells when the plant decays or is burned. The only way a surplus of oxygen can result from photosynthesis is when the carbon is deposited in some long-lasting form or is transformed into something else.

This is, of course, exactly what was happening back in the Permian Period. Much of the lush, green growth on land and sea was being deposited in the earth as coal, gas, and oil—what we call the "fossil fuels." This resulted in the removal of much carbon dioxide from the atmosphere and the release of billions of tons of free oxygen. As we burn these fossil fuels in our furnaces and engines we are using up some of this free oxygen and returning the carbon dioxide to the air. What will happen when we burn all the fossil fuels? Won't we be back where we started, with such a deficiency of oxygen that the atmosphere will no longer support animal life, including human life? Can we learn to breathe a carbon dioxide atmosphere? Not unless we develop chlorophyll cells and become those "little green men" who are supposed to crew the flying saucers.

Fortunately there are other sources of oxygen besides those still unused supplies that are consumed as we burn the fossil fuels. The oceans of the world produce a surplus of oxygen. Few realize that there are more plants in the ocean than on the land. These are mostly microscopic, single-celled plants that float about as plankton near the surface of the seas. These also produce only the amount of oxygen that it takes to consume them by decay, but they don't all decay. Some are constantly sifting down through the water to form an ever-deepening bed of carbon-containing ooze in the deep and comparatively lifeless parts of the oceans. But the oxygen they released remains in our atmosphere for us to breathe.

Another tremendous source of free oxygen is from the amount of carbon tied up at any one time in the trees and other plants of the world. All of these plants, or nearly all, ultimately decay and use up this oxygen—but meanwhile another generation of trees and plants have grown. This is a dynamic process, and the amount of oxygen it furnishes depends on the number and the size of the trees and other plants that are alive, or at least still undecayed, at any given time. How is that for an argument against cutting down our forests?

And, finally, there is one more tremendous source of free oxygen. This is humus, the partly decayed organic matter that makes up the topsoil of the world. There is probably more carbon at any one time in this humus than in all the coal beds of the world. Under natural conditions, when God is doing the organic gardening, this humus or topsoil is gradually deepening and thus more free oxygen is being added to our atmosphere. All too often the picture changes when man comes on the scene.

When the pioneers first cleared the land, the soil was deep, rich, and dark-colored, showing that much carbon was tied up there. But cultivation let oxygen in, and the microscopic life consumes the carbon as it made the plant foods in the humus available to the crops being raised. Bumper crops could be raised with no added plant food, sometimes for many years. But this was depleting the humus in the soil—and the crops taken off were burned by the living cells of the humans and livestock, which consumed them. It makes no difference whether the carbon compounds are burned in the furnace or burned by our own cells as the food we use for energy. The result is the same—oxygen is used and carbon dioxide is released.

Since it is green plants that consume carbon dioxide and release oxygen, one would think that farms would produce a surplus of oxygen, but the vast majority of present-day farms consume more oxygen than they produce. This is because most farms are more humus-mining operations than they are examples of wise agriculture. The organic matter in most farm soil is being depleted rather than built up. This means that the carbon in the humus is being burned—and in burning it uses free oxygen from our atmosphere. Chemical fertilizers merely speed up the process. They ultimately reduce the soil's natural fertility and also destroy its tilth, or workability. Some farmers who have overused chemical fertilizers are already complaining that they have about ten minutes to work the soil between the times it is too wet and too dry.

Real organic farming is not merely refraining from using poisonous sprays and concentrated chemical fertlizers. It could almost be defined as "a method of farming whereby more organic material is returned to the soil than is taken from it." In other words, humus is being built up rather than depleted. Such farming not only gives constantly increasing fertility, tilth, and water-holding power to the soil, but it inevitably results in an oxygen surplus to be added to our deteriorating atmosphere. Other benefits, of course, are more nutritious, healthful, and far better-tasting food.

Universally practiced, this kind of agriculture would solve many of the environmental problems that are now plaguing us. When everyone realizes that all organic (carbon-containing) wastes are valuable, we will return them to the land instead of polluting our streams with them.

A good definition of conservation is "the act of preserving that which is valuable." People simply must be taught that all organic wastes are valuable if returned to the soil. They will actually improve the air.

Your organic garden could have a value you never realized it had. It can not only furnish your family with healthful, nutritious, and good-tasting food, but it may be the leavening that shows the way to a better mode of living, where the environment would be constantly improving, rather than deteriorating. Your demonstrations of the practicality of growing food without harming the land, water, or air may be the key to man's survival on this planet.

16. Are Wild Foods Dangerous?

LETTERS from readers continue to fill my huge rural mailbox at a rate that brings complaints from the mail carrier. Many want information, and I give it when I can—although sometimes I wonder why a specialist in wild plants should be thought a paragon of wisdom on totally unrelated subjects. If a question pertains to domestic plants or gardening, there are much better sources of information than the organic nature lover. I try to be a good organic gardener, but I have too much sympathy with the weeds to be very successful!

The vast majority of letters I get are friendly, but a few are downright hostile. One letter writer commented that all this emphasis on eating wild plants distressed her because not enough warning is given against poisonous plants, and because wild plant gatherers usually trespassed on private property. She was also afraid foragers would deplete the supply of wild plants and maybe even kill off some species entirely. She suggested that those who want such food should grow it themselves or gather it only on their own land.

I do not advocate trespassing. But, once I have explained what I wish to do, I find farmers more than willing that I do it on their land. I have permanent permission to gather wild foods on dozens of farms and woodlands in my area, and can always get permission to use other places if I wish it—and that is certainly not trespassing. Anyone with a reasonable respect for other people's belongings can very easily get such permission.

I do destroy some plants as I gather food from them. Digging dandelion roots, chicory roots, thistle roots, wild carrots, and wild parsnips kills those particular plants, just as you take the lives of similar plants when you gather them in your garden. However, these are all considered pesty weeds by farmers. Besides, they usually grow far too thickly in the wild for their own good, so I'm just giving them a much-needed thinning. Some of my farmer neighbors are going to be very disappointed if I stop digging thistles from their pastures.

There are some good edible wild plants that should not be gathered, and you will never see me advocate their use for food, except maybe for a single experiment or in cases of dire emergency. Foragers are the best of conservationists, because they know the value of the wild places and why they should be protected.

The real menace is the huge array of herbicides sprayed on roadsides, in fields, and over lawns. These are poisons and badly upset the balance of nature. They kill earthworms and wash into streams where they kill aquatic life. Another enemy is the engineering mentality that wants to bulldoze all the hills, fill all the marshes, pave over all open areas—never even knowing the names and natures of the billions of life forms they are destroying.

Wild food gatherers are not just "people who want such food." Wild food gathering is a way of having a creative encounter with nature, and living intimately enough with her to come to know her, love her, and learn her ways. It is a way to change attitudes—from considering nature a menace and an enemy to be conquered, to considering her a friend to be cherished and protected. Nature offers her gifts of food in a gracious manner. It is churlish to refuse them.

Would you suggest to a trout fisherman that he stop fishing and buy his trout in the supermarket? Growing wild food would remove all meaning from the game. Part of the joy is in eating wild food that has been raised by the sweat of no man's brow, nor sold at a profit.

Far from being merely a way to obtain "such food," wild food gathering is primarily an outdoor sport, closely related to hunting and fishing without the gut-wringing twinges of conscience that such activities bring to many of us. It is a superb educational tool, introducing students to nature in a meaningful way, and helping them to develop the attitudes toward nature that they must have if we are to implement the ecological programs we must carry out or perish.

Ecology is the study of life in communities and the interrelationships of such life forms. The best way to teach it is to relate the student to a natural community in a basic way—and I know of nothing more basic than food. Wild food has a symbolic meaning for me; it is the bread and wine in which I have a deep communion with nature and, I believe, with the Author of that nature. To be prejudiced against a food merely because it grows wild is to refuse a gift from God's own organic garden.

My letter-writer said I was not cautious enough about whether or not a plant was edible and gave poke (*Phytolacca americana*) as an example. I have often given my rule whereby a person can be sure of never eating a poisonous wild plant. It is: *Never use any plant for food unless you have positive identification and know it to be an edible species.* I might add: *And also know that the part of it you are eating is wholesome.*

Writers with a "nature-the-menace" outlook often warn us that poke is a poisonous plant. This "poisonous" plant is frequently sold at the food markets of Philadelphia and Lancaster, Pennsylvania, and in many Southern markets for food during its spring season. Young poke shoots, gathered when fat and tender, peeled and cooked like asparagus, could drive asparagus right off the market. The leaves at the tops of the shoots make one of the most delicious cooked vegetables of the spinach type I have ever eaten.

Now, two warnings: First, be sure the plant you are using is really poke. There is a plant sometimes called "Indian poke" in New England that is better called white hellebore (*Veratrum viride*), which contains a harsh drug that lowers the blood pressure dangerously. It is a good medicine in a doctor's hands, but is not for eating nor for the making of home remedies. No one who knows either plant could possibly mistake it for poke, but it is green, attractive, and appears very early in the spring. It has caused severe illness and probably death, though usually the foolish person who has eaten it vomits it spontaneously and thereby saves his life.

Real poke salad or pokeweed also contains a drug (phytolaccin), which is mainly concentrated in the root. These roots are large, succulent, and white on the inside, and some people might be tempted to try them as food. Don't! A very small amount of the dried root is sometimes taken as a home remedy. Meyers in *The Herbalist* recommends putting a tablespoonful of the root in a pint of boiling water, and then taking one teaspoonful of the brew at a dose, but I advise not using it at all. There is probably a tiny bit of this drug in the young shoots. I have, however, eaten many tons of these in my life, and have seen many more tons eaten by other people with no ill effects, so I can safely vouch for their wholesomeness.

I still believe that wild plants are being discriminated against simply because they are wild. There are garden plants that contain poisons in the inedible parts, as well as wild plants. Rhubarb leaf stalks are delicious and wholesome when cooked and sweetened, but the green leaf blades contain enough oxalic acid to be dangerous. Tomatoes, potatoes, and eggplant all produce good food, but the plants, leaves, and stalks contain solanin, a very dangerous alkaloid. Even apples have seeds that are poisonous if eaten in large quantities. And yet no one insists that warnings be given of these dangerous parts every time someone gives a recipe for the use of these common plant foodstuffs.

Another letter, this time a friendly one from a woman in South Carolina who was also worried about poisons in wild plants: The source of her worry is an incredibly erroneous newspaper article with a New York dateline, written, no doubt, by someone with a firsthand unfamiliarity with the facts. A good example of this writing is (and I quote): "The death-dealing wild cherry looks like the harmless domestic variety one buys at the corner fruit stand." I challenge this person to show me that poisonous wild cherry. I have eaten all kinds of wild cherries, in great quantities all of my life, and have suffered no ill effects from them.

I can guess where this error comes from. The foliage of the wild cherry—and the tame one for that matter—develops hydrocyanic acid as it wilts. Wilted cherry leaves have been known to kill livestock. They probably would kill humans too, but I know very few people who habitually eat cherry leaves. The bark of the cherry tree, both the domestic and the various wild cherries, also contain some of this drug; that is why it is used in cough syrups, for tiny amounts of

wild cherry

(*Prunus virginiana*)

hydrocyanic acid can be useful as an expectorant, loosening the phlegm in the thoracic area.

I know there are those who say that they don't want even a tiny amount of any poisonous substance in their system, but that can't be avoided. Did you know that there are many substances which are poisonous in large quantities that your body not only tolerates in small quantities but absolutely must have in order to keep functioning? These include some of the vitamins (essential by definition) and a great many of the minerals.

This same newspaper article reported: "Few people can distinguish a poison variety from an edible one." This, unfortunately, is true, and it betrays the tragic estrangement from nature of our present generation. If we are to save enough of nature to make this earth a decent place on which to live, we must make friends with nature all over again. I know of no better way to get reacquainted with Mother Nature than to accept her invitation to have dinner with her.

17. The Problem of Overconversion

BEING human, I am naturally hurt when people refuse to listen to me—but I am even more deeply troubled when people swallow me whole. I often open a letter and feel gratified to find that I have made a new convert to wild ways, only to read on in dismay that my correspondent is overconverted and is planning ways to put his new enthusiasm into some action that I, with all my years of experience, would be afraid to attempt.

There was a letter from a scoutmaster in Illinois who had read one article in *Organic Gardening* and planned to take thirty-two Boy Scouts to a wilderness area and live for three weeks entirely on wild food with no commercial supplements whatever. He admitted that neither he nor the boys knew one plant from another, nor had they ever had any experience in this line. He wanted me to write and tell him how to do it.

I told him how to do it. I advised that he first go out—alone—for only one day, try to live on wild food, and see how he fared. I would rather have one disillusioned scoutmaster than thirty-two starving scouts permanently turned off to future nature experiences. I wouldn't dream of having thirty-three people live off the land in one group and in one area, even if every one of them had a year's training in wilderness survival. It would be a disaster to the area—a sort of human locust plague.

If I wanted to teach thirty-two Boy Scouts about wild foods and had them in a wilderness area for three weeks, I would be sure that I had ample food supplies along. Then I would spend a week training them on how to recognize, gather without destruction, and prepare the various wild foods of that area and season, adding the ones they found to the regular camp cuisine as special treats. After about two weeks of this, I would set aside one day as the big gathering, send the boys off in small groups to gather certain specific foods, have them all return to camp early so they could spend most of the afternoon cleaning and preparing their bounty, then have one meal of all wild foods.

This experience would point up the areas in which they needed improvement, and when these defects had been honed away by further study and practice I would send them off in pairs, or in very small groups, to spend one day and one night out living off the land, then reward them with a grand feast of the kind of "drive-in" foods that boys adore. I would hope those boys would be inspired to make further experiments on their own with the natural way of life—and that's what education is all about.

A woman from New Jersey wrote that she wanted to surprise the members of her bird-watching club by serving them a complete wild dinner. She wanted me to come down and prepare it for the eighty members of her club. She assured me it would be no trouble, as she had twenty wild acres. She planned to take the club out on a bird-watching

expedition for a few hours and while they were gone I was to
gather and prepare the wild food and be ready to serve the
complete gourmet dinner on their return. She was very
generous, saying that I could use her kitchen, and that she
would pay up to fifty dollars for this service.

I really don't think this letter needs any comment. I
confess that I couldn't prepare a gourmet dinner for eighty
people in an ordinary household kitchen in a few days, let
alone a few hours, even if all the food was delivered to the
door. And, while I'm not rich, I certainly know many easier
ways to earn my keep than that.

A stockbroker called up from our local village and
demanded to see me, pleading that he had driven all the way
from New York. I felt like telling him that I hadn't asked
him to make that drive, and that there were phone lines and
regular U.S. mail deliveries between New York and our
backwoods village, but being a soft-hearted slob I asked him
to come on up.

He was the most overconverted convert I have ever met.
He was understandably fed up with the filth, polluted air,
and traffic jams of New York. A friend had loaned him my
book *Stalking the Wild Asparagus,* and before he finished
reading it he had decided to change his whole way of life. He
planned to quit his job, go to some fruitful wild area, and live
the rest of his life on nothing but wild food. All he wanted
from me was advice on which area would be best for this kind
of life and the knowledge of how it could be done. A short
walk with him convinced me that he not only did not know
one wild plant from another, he didn't even know that plants
were usually composed of roots, stalks, leaves, flowers, and
fruit. He was amazed to discover that flowering had something to do with fruiting and that fruiting had something to
do with seed production and propagation. It was a whole
new world to him.

I tried, as gently as I could, to convince him that as a neoprimitive wild food gatherer he would last about as long as I would as a stockbroker, if I took the job he planned to vacate. His employer would reject me the first day, and nature would reject him just as quickly. I'm sure I have the capacity to become a stockbroker if I were willing to spend the years of study that would be necessary to develop this capacity, and I'm sure he could become a skilled naturalist, able to pluck his food from the wild, at the same price. But for either of us to imagine that we could step into the other's shoes with no preparation is sheer folly.

If all of my letters and visitors were like these I would stop writing, lock my door, and demolish my mailbox. But happily most of my visitors and the writers of most letters I receive are kindred souls with their heads put on the right way. Sometimes I think some of them are overreaching their abilities only because I have underestimated those abilities. A young couple planning a week's sojourn in the wilderness asked me if they could stop by. The wife was a strapping, beautiful specimen of young womanhood with a three-month-old baby in a carrier on her back. I don't mind grownups learning their limitations by hard experience, but I don't want to be a party to starving an infant. I told them that while they would almost certainly survive a week of living on wild food and might even eat well and enjoy it, I knew of too few suitable baby foods to approve of them taking their little one on such a trip. The woman grinned, arched her ample bosom, and asked, "Don't I appear able to feed one tiny child? This baby will get exactly the same food he gets at home. He lives on the most natural food in the world and I produce it."

Recently a letter came with parts of the writing in one

handwriting and parts of it in another. It was from two girls who are approaching wild food in the right way.

Dear Mr. Gibbons:

We have been very busy today. We went to a nearby wild place to forage for all sorts of wild goodies. We picked elder blow, elderberries, crab apples, and milkweed pods. Now our jelly and apple butter are cooling and they sure smell good! Our elder blow fritters disappeared long ago and the milkweed really was good and different.

We both live in Virginia and that is where we first got acquainted with your books. Anita and I are both fifteen and we share a common love for nature. When we get a little older, our dream is to live off the land for about a year. That is why we have read and reread your books.

Last summer we attempted a few days of living off the land. Our main diet was sassafras tea and blueberries. We tried fried daylilies but unfortunately that didn't work out. (We think we had too much oil in the pan.) We got as far as holding the turtle in place, but we couldn't drop the hatchet. Our miserable attempt sent us back to the books.

Now we live in separate environments. Anita is visiting me in Omaha. We have spent the summer experimenting and the last year writing each other of our discoveries.

Between the two of us we have *Stalking the Wild Asparagus, Stalking the Healthful Herbs, How to Survive in the Woods, Wild-Wood Wisdom, Cooking with Flowers, Trees of North America*, and *Plants of the Yellowstone*.

The biggest frustration Nancy and I run into is the unwillingness of people to try something new. So many people (including ourselves) have so many prejudices against strange and different foods. The sad thing is that, not only are people unwilling to try things, but that they also believe that what they have grown up with is best. They miss so much!

Just the other day we were driving along a country road and we spotted some wild plums and mulberries. Nancy has made a mulberry pie already, but the plums were something new to both of us. Also, the day before yesterday we were in this park here in Omaha called Fontanello Forest, and near the Missouri River we found our first wild grapes. They were delicious.

Two weeks ago I went on a back-packing trip in California for five days. We went into the Trinity Alps. They were ruggedly beautiful but I didn't see too many familiar plants. One thing, though, I wish you would tell us, and that is whether or not tiger and leopard lilies are edible. I also made a lot of pennyroyal tea and with honey it was delicious.

Another thing I've been wondering. Do you consider wild foods to be more flavorful than the common sort? Or is it just because we've grown so familiar with common things that they no longer seem new and exotic, just familiar?

Our stonewall right now is the meat course. How are we to capture a creature with edible meat? To us there's something unforgiveable about practicing on an animal when we don't actually need it (yet)! Another thing, if I caught a raccoon I don't think I could eat it—I've had three for pets. What is the most humane way to kill one if you have no gun?

Well, we felt you might be interested in our experience in the wilds. We've gotten to know you a little, we think, through your books, and we hope that through this letter you have come to know us a bit.

Please write if you can.

Sincerely,
Anita and Nancy

Now you can see why I let my mailbox stand. Isn't that a fine letter and aren't they two fine girls? I wish they were my daughters. Even their failures endear them to me. I can't practice on an animal when I don't need it, and it has been years since I had enough heartlessness to let the hatchet drop, though I'm sure I would if I became hungry. The lilies you mention have bulbs that could be eaten, but shouldn't. I'm sure you can be trusted with this information when I tell you that taking the bulb destroys the plant with its promise of another beautiful flower next year. I did get to know you a bit from your letter, but only enough to whet my appetite to know you much better. Please write again.

18. Wild Foods with a College Education

AT THE students' request, I was one of the visiting firemen at the recent Colloquy Weekend at Bucknell University in Lewisburg, Pennsylvania. The committee in charge had invited about seventy well-known "people with ideas" to campus. Classes were adjourned so the students could hear them, question them, challenge them, and be challenged by them. There were groups meeting all over the campus, night and day, on such diverse subjects as Extrasensory Perception, Multi-Media Shows, Non-Objective Film Making, Alternate Life Styles, Sensitivity Training, Black–White Problems, Hypnotism, Ecology and Survival, Wild Foods, and Pollution Problems.

Despite the fact that other interesting things were happening everywhere across the campus at the same time, students came in droves to the wild field trips, films, talks, and demonstrations. Due to the sudden upsurge in concern about our deteriorating environment, the students are turned on to nature in a new and wonderful way. They are no longer satisfied to study biology from books and in laboratories, with an occasional bird walk or wildflower viewing, or any of the other "admire nature from a safe distance" activities of the typical nature-tourist type. They want to get with it, become immersed in nature, and learn its relevance to their own lives and times.

My pet peeve has long been the aesthetic dilettante who simpers, "I love nature more than anything, but I don't know a thing about it." True, one's eyes can take delight in the colors of a wildflower and one's olfactory organ can thrill to its perfume without ever knowing the name of the wild plant that bears it, and even without being able to recognize that plant when it is not in flower. And one can steep one's soul in the music of birdsong without knowing—or even seeing—the birds that are singing. But this is not love of nature, this is love of self, plus sensual indulgence of that self in the titillation of the eyes, nose, and ears that nature freely gives—even to those who "don't know a thing about it."

These students are not of that stripe. They resent the fact that they were raised in a technology-centered culture that ignored nature until man's abuse of it brought him to the brink of disaster. They realize that they know far too little about nature, and this is a situation they are out to correct as quickly as possible. Our modern society has produced neither teachers nor techniques for teaching them what they want to know. They will not be content with leaf collections, long lists of Latin names, and tomes of trivia on classification. They see themselves as a part of all this wonderful creation, and they want to know how the species *Homo sapiens* can become a part of this great interrelatedness of life in a nondestructive manner. Many of them are trying to develop new life-styles that will enable them to live in a more harmonious relationship with nature than man has had in his recent past.

Wild food fascinated them. Along with their concern about the deteriorating environment came a concern about the quality of the dehumanized food that is produced for keeping qualities, shipping qualities, selling qualities, and all the other technological qualities—but not its nutritional qualities. They are suddenly—and very unreasonably in the eyes of some—demanding that we stop producing food to please the packager, the processor, the shipper, and the supermarket, and start producing it to nourish whole and healthy human beings.

They were excited to discover that there are vast stores of nutritious, palatable food raised in God's own organic garden that they could have for the picking. Unlike most groups I have instructed, as soon as these students learned to gather a food plant without being destructive, they started gathering it. Within an hour after returning from the first field trip I was invited to four different wild lunches that had been prepared from the food-gathering that morning.

With their heritage of technological efficiency, they were especially enthusiastic about the wild food plants with multiple uses. The common orange daylily, which always grows so thickly and seems to be begging the passing food-gatherer to thin them out, offered tasty little tubers on its roots—young sprouts that can be peeled and eaten in salads or cooked like asparagus; green buds that can be cooked and served like green beans, or dried to include in some delicious Oriental dishes, or even in plain soups and stews; and even the orange blossoms that can be dipped in fritter batter and fried.

When I explained that the ordinary cattail had edible rhizomes, sprouts, hearts, bloom spikes, and pollen, one of the students said, "Just tell me what you want for dinner and I'll make it from cattails." Burdock that has edible roots, flowerstalks, and leaf stems did a fair job of turning them on, as did dandelions and chicory, which furnish edible crowns, greens, and roots. One can even drink the roots of dandelions and chicory, for when these are roasted and ground they furnish two of the best coffee substitutes in all of nature.

The young people went wild over wild parsnips, Jerusalem artichokes, and wild carrots. Persimmons, wild grapes, black haws, and wintergreen berries were eaten when found—directly from the plants—and everyone nibbled on purflane stems, sheep sorrel leaves, ground cherry fruits, green peppergrass seeds, and other wild tidbits as we walked along. Everyone tasted wild garlic and wild onion—and then we moved on in a cloud of fragrance that would have completely repelled any late arrivals! They enthusiastically dug up groundnuts and hog peanuts to take back to their "pads" and cook.

In the evening we continued our study of wild foods with slides, color films, and questions. This was no passing fancy. These young people had discovered a gap in their knowledge and were determined to make the human race reacquainted with the natural world. They insisted on some kind of follow-up study, and arranged, then and there, another weekend to spend on wild foods later in the fall, this time in a rural setting.

Some parents think only such things as pot-smoking, rioting, shaggy hair, and way-out clothes filter down from the universities to the high schools and grade schools. But good things often travel the same route. Only a few days after the Colloquy, a group of parents concerned about the quality of the outdoor education their children were receiving in the public schools contacted me and asked if I could give the same kind of program in the schools their children attended. The children had heard of it and they were demanding to be turned on to wild food. This put me on a spot! I have deep concern for betterment of outdoor education in the lower

common dandelion

(*Taraxacum officinale*)

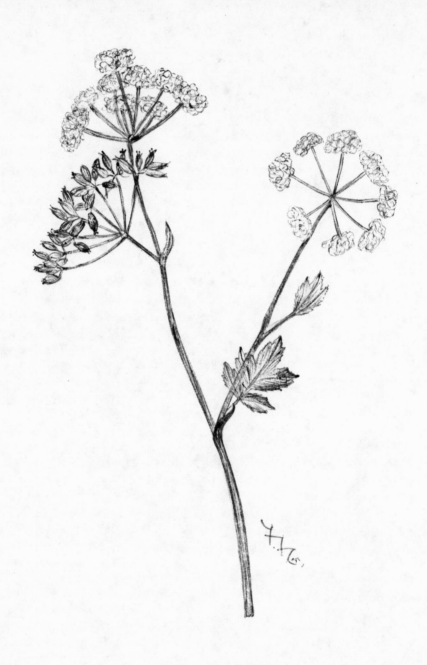

wild parsnip

(*Pastinaca sativa*)

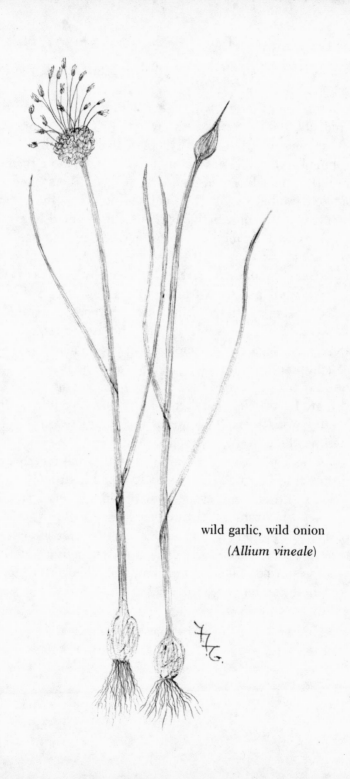

wild garlic, wild onion
(*Allium vineale*)

schools, but I simply haven't the time to take all the local schoolchildren on field trips.

After consultation with the parents, schools, university, students, and especially with my wife—who is a fine teacher —we came up with what I believe to be a really creative solution to this dilemma, and one that solves more than one problem. The Bucknell students, many of them education majors, wanted to put their enthusiasm about the environment to some constructive use, and they wanted to explore creative teaching methods. Most agreed with me that what was needed was a new attitude toward nature to replace the fallacious "conquest of nature" philosophy that has landed us in all this pollution trouble. They also agreed that the place to start is with the children. Then, too, the relationship between Bucknell students and Lewisburg community, though not bad, could stand some improvement.

I proposed to take Bucknell students, ten at a time, on a one-day training expedition. Each participant agreed to take two groups of schoolchildren on a similar expedition during the following week. This meant the material would still be fresh in the university students' minds, and the same plants would still be in season. Some wanted to take even more classes out. We tried to work these expeditions in every few weeks so the student-teachers could both get and give a full seasonal spectrum of nature in this area. This gave the participating students an outlet for their environmental concern, some practice teaching with an unusual method, and the service rendered the community helped to improve student–community relationships.

19. Chesapeake Bay— Why It Won't Die

I'M OFTEN asked by doom-crying ecologists how I can continue to be optimistic about man's future relationships with nature in the face of statistically documented trends showing that conditions are getting worse. Remember, I have been on this ecology kick for a great many years—long before it became so stylish. Mine was once one of a few voices crying in the wilderness. Today that cry is rising to a roar that is covering our whole nation, and it is being heard and heeded in places where something can be done.

One reason for optimism is the existence of organizations like the Chesapeake Bay Foundation and the creative work it is doing. I will state categorically that had such an organization—with Lake Erie as its concern—existed forty years ago we would not today be faced with the tragic death of a great freshwater body on our northern border. There is great joy in knowing that, due to the work of these wonderful people, Chesapeake Bay will not die. Indeed, I fully believe that we will see it gradually recover from the injuries man has inflicted on this beautiful body of water.

The Chesapeake Bay Foundation is a nonprofit organization composed of many different kinds of people with one thing in common: love for the Bay and a desire to see it flourish in all its beauty and usefulness to mankind. The Foundation includes millionaires and hippies, industrialists and beachcombers, sports fishermen and naturalists, scientists and schoolchildren. They are solving the problems of preserving the Bay through a many pronged campaign that includes regional planning, resource management, ecologically sensitive zoning, pollution patrol, field observation and research, natural area registration, water-quality monitoring, environmental education, and a host of self-initiated projects constantly presented by concerned people who are swarming into the group looking for a way to make love visible.

I live more than a hundred miles from the nearest approach of Chesapeake Bay, but several times a year I find myself drawn in that direction for boating, fishing, foraging, or just plain beachcombing. I love this great inland sea and its 3000 miles of shoreline. If this bay is ruined for recreational use, the quality of my life will be diminished. Fortunately, the Bay is far from dead, and although abused and injured in many places with loving care it can completely recover. It still produces thousands of tons of fish, crabs, oysters, and clams. Sport fishermen still throng its waters and a few come back emptyhanded. You can find hundreds of miles of uninhabited shorelines and pristine tidal creeks where you can anchor your boat in primeval solitude or camp in lonely splendor.

An important outreach of the Chesapeake Bay Foundation is its ecological cruises for high school students. Yachtsmen members furnish the boats and naturalist members provide the expertise. The lucky youngsters who participate in such cruises get a wonderful, sugar-coated learning experience that is almost pure, unadulterated fun. When the Foundation asked me to come down and share my wild food enthusiasm on such a cruise, I leapt at the chance.

I love all seasons but I am especially greedy for spring. I have left snowy Pennsylvania and traveled southwest to experience spring in the southern Utah desert. Now I was going to southern Virginia to taste another spring before ours arrived. Going to the rendezvous at Fishing Bay, near the mouth of the Plankatank River, I drove right into spring.

We spent the evening at the yacht club, discussing our plans, and studying color slides of the edible plants we expected to find along these shores. Enthusiasm ran high for this new way of relating to their lovely bay.

Next morning while the boats were gassing up, I took some students into an adjoining field where we gathered poke (*Phytolacca americana*), dock (*Rumex crispus*), cleavers (*Galium aparine*), dandelion greens (*Taraxacum officinale*), and a host of other wild spring vegetables. Then we were out on the bright water of Plankatank River, and we skimmed up to a beautiful, uninhabited island covered with groves of persimmon and pine.

We had been warned that this tidal inlet offered no shellfish, but we were barely ashore when we saw that the saltmarsh was alive with striated mussels (*Modiolus demissus*) and marsh periwinkle (*Littorina irrorata*). Although neither of these creatures is commonly eaten, both can furnish wholesome food to those not allergic to molluscan shellfish. We gathered a supply. Cat brier or green brier (*Smilax rotundifolia*) was all too plentiful in the bushy parts of the island. New sprouts and leaf buds furnished a wild salad that was highly appreciated by the young foragers. There was more poke around abandoned campsites, and along the trails

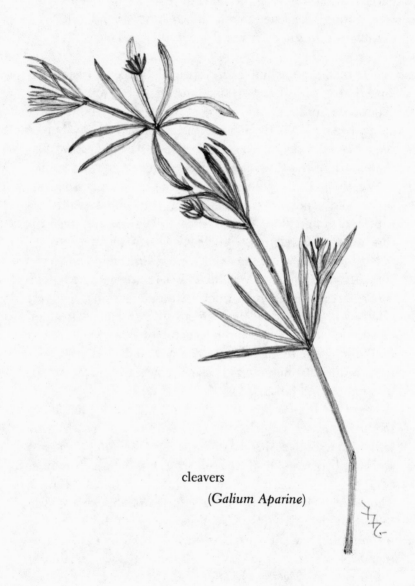

cleavers

(*Galium Aparine*)

we found all the sheep sorrel (*Rumex acetosella*) we could use. Our food hoard grew.

We added various wild greens to our sandwich lunch, then headed for the adjacent mainland to do some exploring. There we found some of the same seaside plants I have enjoyed on the Maine Coast: sea rocket (*Cakile edentula*) and orach (*Atriplex patula*). A walk up in the fields gave us all the cress we cared to gather, besides furnishing more poke, dock, and other spring greens. Returning through the woods we found the angelica tree (*Aralia spinosa*), commonly called devil's-walking-stick or Hercules'-club, in great abundance. This spiny shrub grows a great panicle of large, compound leaves every spring. I had long heard that these leaves were edible if caught in exactly the right stage—when just unrolling with the prickles still soft and tender—but this was the first time I had ever found them in that condition, so we helped ourselves to a good supply. They had a pleasant, aromatic flavor raw and gave promise of being a good vegetable cooked. A member of the famous ginseng family so highly valued by the Orientals, this shrub is supposed to restore lost youth and lengthen life. I needed a good shot of it, for these energetic youngsters were running me ragged.

We followed a trail through the woods and came on the ruins of a great antebellum plantation. A magnificent mansion was falling apart, its roof and floors gone, and a great patch of poke growing before the ornate fireplace in the huge living room. There were sunken gardens, overgrown box hedges, and other signs of luxurious and opulent living now long vanished. In a little brick-walled family graveyard we found tombstones dating back to long before the Revolution.

Amid all this faded glory a myriad of wild food plants grew in great abundance. We gathered more poke and winter cress and dug a great supply of burdock roots (*Arctium minus*). A

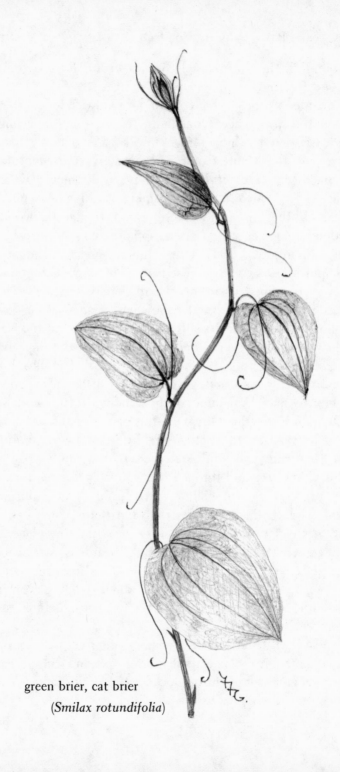

green brier, cat brier
(*Smilax rotundifolia*)

orach

(*Atriplex patula*)

Hercules'-club

(*Aralia spinosa*)

vegetable highly valued by the Japanese, burdock is another food that's supposed to revivify the old, refresh the tired, restore the energyless, and fortify the weak. Scraped and cut crosswise like carrots, then boiled until tender and seasoned with butter and salt, they do make a good, starchy, potatolike food.

The lower end of a sunken garden had become marshy and had grown up in cattails. We peeled the young stalks to get the tender hearts—so good in salads or boiled as a mild, sweet vegetable. We also dug a bagful of sassafras roots to make tea for the wild party we were planning.

All day we had tried to convince somebody to go fishing for some protein food to complement our wild vegetables, but everyone was so turned on with wild-food gathering that they refused to stop for anything so mundane as ordinary angling. When we first landed on the mainland I had noticed that the shallow bottom was covered with razor clam shells (*Tagelus gibbus*), so upon returning to the boats I suggested that we try to capture some of the live ones. The stout razor doesn't just lie still and let you dig him up as a respectable edible clam is supposed to do. He lives in a burrow into which he can quickly slide down until out of reach, and if you try digging down to him he simply escapes through the sand.

But these smart youngsters soon proved capable of outwitting wily clams by suddenly thrusting one hand down into the sand and holding their victims still until they could dig them out with the other hand. These are delicious clams and we soon had enough to make a difference in the wild meal we were planning. The young people were having too much fun to stop and the sun went down before they had their fill of this activity. We returned to the island laden with a wealth of wild food.

As night closed in I felt apprehensive. After such a glorious

burdock

(*Arctium minus*)

day, I was afraid that we had exhausted the interest span of
these youngsters and that the end of the day would frazzle
away, but I had underestimated my crew. They set up a camp
on the island and began cleaning and cooking everything we
had brought in. I simply stood by—or rather I lay on a soft
bed of pine needles—and acted solely in an advisory
capacity. We didn't have a regular meal, but as each dish was
prepared we ate it, exclaimed and enthused over it, then we
went on to the next course. The wild meal lasted five hours.
Then with everyone stuffed and happy we slept under the
stars.

Next morning the students learned how to monitor water
quality, testing it for turbidity, bacteria content, and exploring several other ways in which to judge how well the Bay was
standing up under the impact of man. They also demanded
another field trip so they could carry some of the wild
delicacies they had sampled back to their friends who had
missed this trip.

Finally, we had an informal evaluation of the cruise, and it
was with deep joy that I discovered that these boys and girls
were dedicated to seeing that Chesapeake Bay doesn't suffer
the fate of some other bodies of water in this country. They
knew why they wanted the Bay saved, for now they had
formed a real relationship with it that promised to enrich
their lives. Plans for future creative encounters with this Bay
and its shores were already in the air. I drove back to
Pennsylvania feeling good about the future of the Chesapeake Bay and the future of this group of fine young people
who had shared a wonderful weekend with me. As if sharing
my mood, I found that spring had come to Pennsylvania
during my absence.

If you live in the Chesapeake Bay area, or even if you just
travel there occasionally, and would like to be a part of the
wonderful work the Chesapeake Bay Foundation is doing,

their address is 17 State Circle, Box 1709, Annapolis, Maryland 21404. If you have a concern for the preservation and improvement of the environmental integrity of Chesapeake Bay they will be glad to hear from you.

20. Loving Unseen Nature

BIOLOGY is basic. It's any society's views on the essence of nature that largely determine that society's decisions and behavior. It makes no difference that the deciders and doers are usually totally unaware of this influence. If fallacious beliefs about the nature of living things are generally accepted in any group, then that group's decisions and behavior will be wrong. I maintain that most of the ills from which our own society suffers have their origin in a cluster of widely accepted biological fallacies. If these views of nature continue to prevail, then we are headed for an ultimate disaster.

Evolutionary progress is made through natural selection, governed by the survival of the fittest in the struggle for existence. All nature is an arrangement of adversary systems contending with one another. In this primal struggle the victor survives and the defeated becomes extinct. Aggression is a law of nature. Power and the will to use it against competitors is the key to survival.

181

I trust that even the persons who hold these beliefs agree that this is an honest and fair statement. I am convinced that basing our decisions and behavior on these beliefs is the road to destruction.

How can a vaguely held biological belief affect our lives to any extent? Actually it affects nearly every decision made that influences our lives. For example, a decision must be made whether or not to fill in a salt marsh and erect a housing development on the fill. Any biologist can explain that this will mean the death of thousands of life forms and untold billions of individual organisms, and will adversely affect the life-carrying capacity of the adjacent ocean. But will these facts alter the decision? Are not these "competing" life forms using space that we want and need? In the same way these false beliefs will affect the decisions to build dams, highways, and canals, drain swamps, level mountains, build jetports, and all other "beneficial public works."

In agriculture these beliefs lead to the use of broad-spectrum insecticides that slaughter the innocent and the beneficial along with the actual pests. Believing that we are engaged in the "conquest of nature" we can't be bothered that these poisons also decimate wildlife and fish, pollute streams, and leave residues in our food to endanger our own health. These are the price of victory in our war on nature. We indiscriminately use herbicides in weed control and are not even deterred by a container's proud claim that this same chemical can be used to eradicate earthworms!

Recently a well-known and highly respected publisher (in a speech to the detergent manufacturers' convention) stated that he is not at all dismayed that man will cause the extinction of more than a hundred species in this century. Isn't this a law of nature? Doesn't the fact that they will become extinct prove that these species are unfit—undeserving of continued existence? He labeled all ecologists and conservationists who are desperately trying to save and improve the quality of our environment as soft-headed sentimentalists who think more of whooping cranes and honey bees than they do of humans.

A weekly news magazine published a progress report on "man's war with insects," proudly reporting new weapons that were being developed to use against these enemies of mankind. The writer obviously believed that man's chances of survival would be enhanced if all insects could be eliminated. Quite the contrary, man could starve. We are totally dependent on insects to pollinate a large percentage of the food crops on which we survive.

In foreign policy, how much do the false beliefs affect the decision to use the ultrapowerful weapons that are only slightly less destructive than nuclear weapons? Their area of destruction is so widespread that any attempt to use these bombs against enemies is certain to result in the deaths of vast numbers of noncombatants. But are not these innocents also at least potential competitors for the means of subsistence, and is not our chance of survival increased by their deaths?

In medicine, how much have these false beliefs influenced the development and use of modern "shotgun" remedies, making even careful diagnosis unnecessary? I recently suffered from a serious bronchial infection with a high fever. My doctor made no attempt to determine the exact cause of my illness, but prescribed ampicillin—one of the most powerful of the "shotgun" medicines—explaining that it killed such a broad spectrum of organisms that it was almost certain to get the "bug" that was causing my trouble. It did. I immediately recovered from the illness, but almost died from the remedy. The same doctor then explained that the medicine had cut such a murderous swath through my system that it had not only killed the offending organism but had also eradicated the lactobacilli that reside in my intestinal tract and perform functions there that are vital to me. He put me on a diet of unpasteurized buttermilk to restore this symbiotic intestinal flora without which I could not survive.

I recently saw an ad for a disinfectant that bragged, "Science proves that our product will kill millions of bacteria in just fifteen seconds!" Why did the ad man feel certain that this blurb would appeal to readers and help sell the product? Because he knew that the vast majority of readers accepted as axiomatic that man and bacteria are two adversary systems in a life-and-death battle for survival. He believes it himself. After all, bacteria cause dozens of diseases in man and in his domestic animals and food crops. Man would be vastly better off if all bacteria were dead. Right?

Wrong, wrong, disastrously wrong! Without bacteria there would be no decomposition. We would have to climb over the trunks of all the trees that ever grew, stumble over the bodies of all of the dead animals that ever lived, and wade through all the sewage ever produced. But of course we wouldn't have to do these things—for without bacteria there would never have been any trees, any animals, any sewage, or us. I could fill a book with examples of why all higher life is totally dependent for survival on bacteria, but one is enough. Without bacteria there would be no fertile soil, therefore no green plants to capture the energy with which we all are powered.

The numbers in which bacteria exist boggle the imagination. If you take a handful of rich, damp soil from your organic garden, you are probably holding a billion bacteria. Try to figure the bacterial population of your whole garden. Think of the other billions living in non-soil media. These organisms are so small that it would take about 100 million of them to fill a teaspoon and this number would weigh about one-tenth of an ounce. And yet the combined weight of all bacteria in the earth's biosphere would probably exceed that of all other living things put together. A very few species of this multitude are injurious to man, most of the others are beneficial, while no small number are utterly essential to man's continued survival.

A cow can't digest hay. If we could remove all the bacteria from a cow, then feed her hay from which all the bacteria has been removed, she would promptly starve to death. A cow licks in hay in fairly uniform mouthfuls, wads it into compact, round balls mixed with her mouth juices and inoculated with bacteria, then slides them into her rumen. The bacteria find the rumen an ideal habitat, warmed to body heat, supplied with food in great quantities, and just the right amount of moisture. Under such benign conditions bacteria double their number every half hour. Let's say there are a million bacteria in each little cud by the time it settles into the rumen, a very conservative estimate. In only three hours they will not only have vastly altered the hay into a more digestible form, but will have multiplied to about sixty-four million bacteria.

A termite can't digest wood. I have written before about the protozoan that lives in the termite's digestive tract and digests cellulose for its host. Science has recently taken another look at this interesting creature, this time under the electron microscope that magnifies it several hundred times larger than it had ever been seen before. Lo and behold, it is not an "it" but a "them." It was formerly thought to be a fairly ordinary flagellate protozoan, noted mainly for the speed with which it could swim through the termite's gut, gobbling up the finely chewed bits of wood constantly supplied by his host. Now it appears that those flaggellates are not flaggellates at all but separate animals—fully formed, perfect spirochetes that attach themselves to the larger protozoans and exchange motive power for a share of the nutriments in the cellulose. What kind of communication exists between these spirochetes that enables them to beat in synchrony with such efficiency that their host became noted for its speed?

There are little oval "organelles" inbedded in the surface near the point of attachment of the spirochetes. These, under supermagnification, we see to be our old friends the bacteria, probably having some function in the care and feeding and the harnessing of the spirochetes. In the transparent, liquid innards of the chief protozoan of this assemblage are seen still other bacteria, drifting around with the still-undigested wood chips. It just may be that this cellulose-digesting protozoan who has been so highly praised as a classic example of symbiosis is a lovable fraud. Maybe he can't digest wood any better than his host termite can, and depends on his symbiotic bacteria in the same way the cow does. However the digestion is accomplished, it is done with high efficiency, enabling the protozoan to maintain itself, a stable of spirochetes, two herds of bacteria, and still keep its termite host furnished with enough energy to eat my house.

Science is now assembling a considerable body of evidence to substantiate that it was some such assemblage of creatures that fused to form the sophisticated cell types that, by further cooperation, came together to form the multicelled life forms, a process that has already culminated in such wondrous creatures as flowers, fruit, furry animals, and you. Does this sound like the survival of the fittest in a competitive struggle for existence? Far from nature being an Ishmaelite battle of everything-against-everything, it now appears that it is in the nature of living things to cooperate, pool resources, and coalesce where possible. This, at last, gives us a reasonable way of accounting for the progressive enrichment and complexity of form in living things.

21. The Perfect Power Plant

IF CIVILIZATION is to continue it must find either an inexhaustible energy source—or a renewable one. Our present technological and industrial civilization is largely powered by fossil hydrocarbons such as coal, petroleum, and natural gas. Our supply of them is definitely limited in quantity, nonrenewable, and being depleted at an alarming rate. We extract power from the energy-carrying hydrocarbons by oxidation—easily accomplished by setting the hydrocarbon on fire—and make use of the heat energy produced to run our automobiles, generate our electricity, and heat our homes.

When a hydrocarbon molecule is oxidized by burning, the molecule is torn violently apart and its carbon and hydrogen atoms combine separately with oxygen atoms from the air, forming two different molecules. Hydrogen and oxygen combine to make plain, ordinary water. Carbon and oxygen team up to form carbon dioxide. A few other things also occur—as city smog testifies—but this is how a pure, perfectly burned hydrocarbon would end up. Even with our impure hydrocarbons and imperfect combustion, nearly all the fuel we burn becomes water and carbon dioxide. Such a method of powering civilization not only depletes our limited supply of fossil fuels, but also ties up oxygen from the air in forms that make it unavailable for either breathing or running engines.

The fact that this supply of fossil fuels under the surface of the earth is complemented by an oxygen-rich atmosphere above it is not coincidental. Experts agree that the earth's atmosphere once contained much less oxygen and more carbon dioxide. Ancient plants, using solar power, tore apart the molecules of water and carbon dioxide, then recombined the carbon and hydrogen into hydrocarbon fossil fuels with some of the solar energy built into them. A by-product of this process was free oxygen, but just enough oxygen to reduce these hydrocarbons to water and carbon dioxide again when they are burned. Since nature chose to place these unburned hydrocarbons into long-term, underground storage, we have had extra oxygen around to breathe. How much free oxygen will remain in the atmosphere if we burn all the fossil fuels?

It is true that this oxygen once belonged to carbon-and-hydrogen atoms in our fossil fuels, and we have had it only on a long-term loan. This is a debt we cannot afford not to repay. We have adjusted our life processes to this borrowed oxygen. If the mortgage is foreclosed and the oxygen taken away, we will perish.

Must we then give up burning hydrocarbon molecules as an energy source? Not if we can find a way to manufacture as many as we use, so the supply stays constant. Many kinds of high-energy molecules can be assembled from hydrogen and carbon and such molecules have many advantages as energy sources. The raw materials are plentiful, for two-thirds of our world is covered with water (which is oxidized hydrogen) and there is plenty of carbon dioxide around. Energized molecules of carbon and hydrogen contain concentrated power, are easily portable, convenient to store, and—best of all— when they are used, only the energy is removed. The carbon and hydrogen go right back into the general supply to be recycled. Moreover, the manufacturing process of energizing these molecules liberates as much oxygen as is needed to free that energy when we get ready to use it, so we would not deplete our oxygen supply by a single atom.

The energy contained in an energized hydrogen-carbon molecule doesn't appear by magic. It must come from some outside energy source. If we are to manufacture such molecules for use as our energy requirements, we need an inexhaustible, nonpolluting energy source that doesn't use up oxygen nor deplete our precious, limited resources. Impossible as it sounds, we already have such an energy source. It is the constant stream of heat and light energy pouring on the earth from the sun.

What is needed is a solar-powered factory that can tear apart the energyless molecules of water and carbon dioxide, recombine the hydrogen and carbon atoms into some high-energy form, and at the same time release into our atmosphere as much new free oxygen as it will take to release the stored energy. This factory should have a more sophisticated automation than any we have been able to devise, being self-adjusting and self-repairing. Furthermore, it should have a built-in construction department so we won't have to build new factories. To power some of these auxiliary operations we could allow the factory to use some of the fuel it produces, but there must be a net surplus that we can use for our own energy needs. Finally, it must not be an eyesore, but instead add beauty to the landscape.

Does this sound like some illusory dream of perpetual motion? The factory I describe, meeting all the conditions laid down, already exists. Except for a few minor applications of wind and water power, it furnished the whole world's energy needs until the invention of the heat engine. It is every green plant in the world.

Such a marvelous factory certainly deserves a closer look than most people ever give it. This factory not only builds itself, but manufactures its own building material. A friend and I were admiring a majestic hemlock in an area of virgin timber near my home. He picked up a handful of dirt from the forest floor and remarked, "Isn't it miraculous that such a magnificent tree can be made from material like this?" I said, "You'd be surprised how little of this material was used in the construction of that tree." He asked, "How can that be? Doesn't that tree live on plant foods from this soil?" I had to answer, "No. It lives on pure sugar, which it manufactures in its leaves. It borrows tiny amounts of minerals from the soil, but these are really tools, not food, as they are not turned into energy. If this tree is allowed to live out its life, die, and decay here, it will return those borrowed minerals down to the last atom."

Some 300 years ago a Dutch physician, J. B. van Helmont, proved that plants don't eat dirt, but a great many people do not know this important fact and still think a tree is fed by its roots on food taken from the soil. The good doctor weighed exactly 200 pounds of soil, put it into a barrel, and planted a young willow that weighed exactly five pounds in it. He watered and tended the willow for five years, then carefully removed it—and found that it had gained 164 pounds. He then weighed the soil and found that it had lost only two ounces of weight! All but two ounces of that tremendous weight gain had been due to materials the tree had made from high-energy sugar molecules manufactured from water and atmospheric carbon dioxide, using solar energy for power and some of these same sugar molecules for the energy required in the building. I wonder how long it would have taken to convince that doctor that a sizable part of the mysterious weight gain he had observed was made from the carbon dioxide in his own exhaled breath as he tended the tree.

I don't want to downgrade roots. While they don't feed a tree, they do collect water for it, and a tree is a most intemperate drinker. On a hot summer's day, a deciduous tree in full leaf may need as many as 900 gallons of water. To supply this quantity, the roots must constantly move by growing new root hairs to capture water from every grain of soil it can reach. The tree can actually grow miles of new root hairs every day. When we look at a tree, we are seeing only half its total bulk. The rest is underground.

How is this great quantity of water transported up the tree to where it is needed? The tree, and for that matter all land plants, have a clever, efficient plumbing system. The piping is made of long, slender cells that grow end to end. As soon as they are mature, the insides are removed, leaving tiny, continuous pipes running all the way from the outer end of the roots to the topmost leaf of the tree. Every growing season the tree adds thousands of new pipes, while some of the old lines, nearer to the center of the tree, fall into disrepair. But where does the power come from to pump all that water to the top of my 150-foot hemlock? Do the roots pump it that high?

Roots do pump, after a fashion. The root cells that collect moisture can become so turgid that the water inside is under considerable pressure. Have you ever seen evenly spaced water droplets around the margin of a strawberry leaf on an early morning after a dewless night? This phenomenon, called guttation, is the result of root pressure pushing more water into the leaf than it can evaporate. It demonstrates that root pressure can get water to the top of a plant a few inches high. But such pressure can't help my tree, for its first leaf is far higher than root pressure can push water under the very best conditions. Besides, when a tree is using water fastest and needs it most, roots have negative pressure; that is, they are actually sucking rather than pushing.

Could the twigs and leaves in the treetop form a partial vacuum and suck the water up the little pipes the same as we suck malted milk through a soda straw? The twigs and leaves do suck when part of their water is lost through evaporation. But any schoolboy can tell us that a suction pump can't lift water more than about thirty-two feet, and my hemlock has thirsty foliage more than a hundred feet higher than that.

Is the energy furnished by the living cells? That is, does the energy come from burning part of the carbohydrate fuel the tree is producing? It won't wash. The cells that make up the waterworks of the tree are empty, dead cells. The tree has no equivalent of the animal heart, no pump made of living tissue, no booster, no moving parts. It can be shown that once the plumbing system is in operation not a single living cell puts out a single calorie of energy in getting water up the tree.

The tree, by making an exquisite adjustment to the peculiar properties of water, air, and heat, has set up a completely automatic water pump, powered with solar heat that furnishes it with all the water it needs. A seventy-foot oak was cut down and soaked in a vat of acid until the experimenters were certain that all cells were dead. The oak was then put back upright, its base in water, and its water supply system continued to operate as it did when the tree was alive.

A tree really has two plumbing systems, almost completely independent of one another. After the little chlorophyll factories in the leaves make sugar from the hydrogen-and-carbon atoms that the tree steals from air and water, this sugar must be transported to the cells that need fueling for new growth, flowering, fruiting, seed-bearing, water collecting, and other energy-using activities. The sugar is in a solution transported by pipelines in the thin, living layer of bark just outside the woody part of the tree trunk. This time the pipelines are composed of living cells—and this makes them very difficult to study, for any attempt to observe them in action throws them out of action.

The living sugar pipelines are so small, so delicate, and surrounded by so much intercellular liquid that it is almost impossible to get even one pure sample of their contents. So when you have a little job in confined space, hire a little worker. The tiny aphid obviously has no difficulty in getting at this sugar solution. He has a built-in soda straw, long enough to reach from the surface of the bark to the sugar pipes.

A clever scientist noticed all of this and snipped an aphid loose from his stylet, which is what scientists call the soda straw. He found that the severed stylet, with its other end still immersed in the sugar solution, kept exuding droplets for days. These could be sucked up in micropipette and analyzed. They were found to contain from ten percent to thirty percent sugar. Today, all samples of this sugar solution needed for study are collected by using this organic tool furnished by the tiny aphid.

I could go on for volumes cataloging the wonders to be seen when closely observing these green plant carbohydrate factories. But maybe just a few will convince you that these wonderful organisms are worth studying. Today every ten-year-old can tell you how an automobile operates, yet very few of our best-educated adults have any idea how the green cell of a plant operates. These cells must collect from the sun all the energy that our food contains, and at the same time keep our air breathable. Recently, and very suddenly, man had come into control of enough power to seriously disrupt or even totally destroy these basic processes on which our very lives depend. Can we afford to blunder on in our ignorance? When will we learn that the perfect industrial plant is a green plant, and start building our own technology on this marvelous model?

22. The Facts of Life

A FATHER called on the principal of the school his son
attended and complained: "My boy has been in this
school seven years and he still doesn't know anything about
the bees and flowers."

The principal probed, "Do you mean that we haven't been
teaching your son about sex?"

The father exploded, "He knows more about sex than I
do. But he still doesn't know anything about the bees and
flowers!"

This echoes my own complaint against much of modern
education. Things are improving, but I still find far too many
students (and teachers too, for that matter) who are not even
aware that we are totally dependent—both for the food we
eat and the air we breathe—on the tiny, chlorophyll-bearing
cells of green plants.

To live, to move, to grow, to reproduce requires energy.
The energy that supports life has only one source, the sun.
The only life form that can directly utilize this energy is the

chlorophyll-bearing plant cell. All other life forms have to get their sun energy secondhand from these plants.

The process by which plants turn out energy into chemical energy is photosynthesis. Asking how photosynthesis is achieved is a bit like asking how life began. We don't know. Man, with all his vaunted science, has never been able to reproduce this process in a test tube. We are only beginning to understand a little about this process on which our very lives depend. Somehow, light on the green pigments in plant cells furnishes enough power to tear apart the hydrogen-and-oxygen atoms of water molecules. The oxygen is released into the atmosphere, then the hydrogen combines with carbon dioxide from the air and forms sugar. This is the most basic of all basic industries—for each of these little sugar molecules is a concentrated pill of energy. This energy—that builds and powers all of life—is released whenever the sugar recombines with exactly the same amount of oxygen that was released during its manufacture. Only the green plants can create their own power source. For all other forms of life—including you and me—the power to live and be, to grow and do, must come from the green plants. There is no other source.

With the exception of green plants, all life lives on life, or on the organic products of life. Inside the microscopic green-pigmented plant cell is the only place in nature where we encounter the miracle of creation; inorganic minerals become living organic compounds. Although these cellular sugar factories are so tiny that there may be fifty million of them on a single green leaf, this is not only the most important industry in the world; it is by far the largest. When we see the superhighways, parking lots, shopping centers, and urban sprawl now rapidly covering God's green earth, we might think the cement industry is larger. But all the cement plants in the world together turn out only about 590 million tons of cement per year. That is enough to cause great

dismay in the ecologist, but puny production when compared to the amount of sugar manufactured by those little
green cells. All the plants in the world produce at least 150
billion tons of sugar each year, or more than 250 times the
cement total.

I'm sure many health food enthusiasts are aghast at the
idea that all life lives on sugar. But sugar is merely the basic
building block and energy cell. Other life forms—including
the other cells in the very plants that made the sugar in the
first place—can perform miracles of alteration, although they
can't create. They can recombine the sugar with oxygen—
that is, burn it—to produce energy used to combine this
organic sugar into unbelievably complex, organic molecules
of protein, fat, other kinds of carbohydrates, and other
compounds necessary to life. This is where sugar belongs, not
in your diet. We can live better and longer on the other
organically produced compounds than if we try living on the
original sugar from which they were made.

It is awe inspiring to think that all plant life, from
one-celled vegetative plankton floating aimlessly in the
currents of the sea, to the giant sequoia—as well as all animal
life, from the amoeba to the great blue whale—owe their life
and form to the single product of the little green plant cell.
In these living things we find thousands of different struc-
tures and compounds, but the basic building block of them
all was sugar. The energy it took to construct these marvelous
life forms was all furnished by the combustion of this same
sugar. We live in a sweet world.

Let's examine that energy. It takes energy—quite a lot of it
considering the size of the task—to tear apart water-and-car-
bon-dioxide molecules. When the component atoms are
recombined into sugar molecules, this energy is an unseen
ingredient—which is released when your body breaks down
the sugar molecules and atoms combine with oxygen to once

again form water and carbon dioxide. It is this stored energy on which all living things operate.

Originally, all the energy I use came from the sugar produced by green-pigmented plant cells. To these lowly cells I owe my ability to move my fingers while typing this chapter, or to pace the floor while thinking. And I owe them the energy for those unconscious tasks that support life, like keeping my body heated to approximately 98.6 degrees F. regardless of temperature of the room where I am working, beating my heart to keep a blood supply coursing through me, and even lifting my ribs to inhale the air that furnishes the oxygen that combines with the sugar's carbon and hydrogen to cause it to burn—in turn releasing the energy that enabled me to lift my ribs in the first place.

Plants, even those that manufacture these energy cells, must also use a certain amount of energy. True, they don't walk the floor or type manuscripts, but it takes energy to raise the tons of timber high above the ground that one sees in the mighty redwood trees. The plant gets its energy from exactly the same source that I get mine. Only the chlorophyll cells are powered by the energy of light, and even these are powered in this fashion only for the photosynthetic process. All other power the plant needs to perform its simple tasks it gets—as I do—by burning sugar in its cells.

Right here I would like to clear up one widely held fallacy. Photosynthesis is not respiration. I was trying to impress a schoolboy with the importance of photosynthesis to all life and he said, "Oh yes, I know all about that. My teacher told me that animals breathe oxygen and exhale carbon dioxide, while plants breathe carbon dioxide and exhale oxygen." Sometimes ignorance is not so much not knowing things as it is knowing so many things that simply aren't true. This is one of the things many people know that isn't true.

It is true that the green cell takes in air, removes carbon

from it, and releases oxygen, but this is a shoveling of raw material into its little sugar factory and has nothing to do with breathing. The plant does breathe, for exactly the same reason that you and I breathe, to take in oxygen to burn carbon and hydrogen, to make the energy that the plant needs to perform the work it must do to grow and stay alive. The waste products from this burning are exactly the same ones I exhale—carbon dioxide and water vapor. How fortunate for us that the plant doesn't do more strenuous human activities, or otherwise use large amounts of energy, for then there would be no surplus sugar and oxygen for us.

Free, uncombined oxygen is the only kind that can be used for breathing. Only free oxygen will support combustion. When combined with hydrogen, as in water, or with carbon, or as in carbon dioxide, it becomes a nonflammable substance that is used to fill fire extinguishers. All the free oxygen in our atmosphere originally came from photosynthesis in tiny green plant cells.

Since plants free only enough oxygen to burn the carbon and hydrogen contained in the sugar they produce, it would seem impossible that a surplus could ever build up to make an oxygen-containing atmosphere, such as surrounds our planet. This would be true if all carbon and hydrogen found in plant matter were recombined with oxygen, but fortunately some of it is stored. The great oil-and-coal deposits under the earth are no more than carbon and hydrogen from prehistoric plants, so even automobiles and furnaces run on energy originally taken from the sun by green plant cells. The humus in topsoil and the organic ooze that covers the bottoms of deep oceans contain vast quantities of carbon and hydrogen.

Much of the carbon and hydrogen is tied up for long periods in living things, or products of living things, that have not yet been burned, metabolized, or decayed. For every two atoms of hydrogen so tied up there is one atom of oxygen loose in our atmosphere; and for every atom of carbon dioxide there are two atoms of oxygen loose in our atmosphere for us to use for breathing. What happens if we burn all the oil and coal, destroy the humus of the soil by using only chemical fertilizers, cover all the places where wild plants can grow with concrete, and poison the sea with runoff from pesticides until it will no longer support plant life? The answer is easy. We die.

Why do I feel that it is necessary to know these facts of life? As one high school student pointed out to me, photosynthesis went on fine for millions of years before we knew about it. The sad fact is that, while nature took excellent care of all this in the past, we have just reached the point where nature cannot take care of it in the future unless we come to her rescue. Already the oxygen levels in crowded cities are dropping dangerously low. Traffic directors on busy intersections in Tokyo have to carry supplementary oxygen to breathe in order to keep their own life processes going.

This knowledge has become vital to our survival. We need new attitudes toward nature and her processes. It is all very well to love nature because of beautiful bird songs and pretty flowers, but won't we have more concern when we realize that we must protect nature or perish? When we know that seventy percent of the oxygen renewing our atmosphere comes from plants that grow in the sea, will we sit idly by while an arrogant military dumps radioactive wastes and poisonous gas into the oceans, thus endangering their capacity to grow plants? Won't we become outraged when we see spray trucks destroying vegetation by roadsides, creating runoff problems that might destroy life in the waters of the earth? Won't we turn to farming methods that build, rather than destroy, the humus content of topsoil? Won't we rise up and cry, "Halt!" to those who would cover every space with concrete?

23. What Ecology Is All About

IT IS a maddening paradox that, while the word ecology is becoming a widely known term, it's meaning is being lost. Most students seem to know vaguely that it has something to do with the environment. They might even hazard a guess that an ecologist is some kind of conservationist, but few can give a more precise definition. Considered etymologically, the word literally means "study of the home," which doesn't tell us much. In the biological sciences it is usually defined as "the study of life in communities," but I find this unsatisfactory. I have yet to find a totally isolated and independent community of life forms—not even those strange and protected communities of life one finds on small, distant islands, in deep caves, or in the isolated water holes of the desert. All such life communities are connected to other life groups by many links. There is really only one community, one vast web of life that extends over the whole face of the earth. For convenience, we sometimes think of distinct communities of life, but the boundaries of such communities exist in the ecologist's mind, not in nature. The really learned ecologist could trace relationships between the luminescent angler fish from the sea's depths to the kangaroo rat hopping along the Continental Divide in arid New Mexico. The definition of ecology that I like best is "the study of the interrelationship of all life forms."

What good is it? How does such an abstraction affect our daily lives and the quality of the environment in which we live? The mighty Charles Darwin, with his tongue partly in his cheek, once explained this. When Britannia ruled the waves, Darwin made the astonishing statement that it was due to the large number of old maids who lived in English villages that England was able to control the seas of the world. The doughty British tar was admittedly the best seagoing fighting man in the world, but his doughtyness and his battling abilities came from the way he was fed, on the good red beef of old England. This meat received its goodness from the way the cattle were fed—on the good red clover of English pastures and hay meadows. To produce seed, red clover must be pollinated, and this can be done by only one insect, the bumblebee. Bumblebees are preyed on by field mice, and, unless the field mouse population was kept under control, bumblebees would soon be exterminated. Fortunately, field mice were preyed on by common house cats who wander the fields around English villages at night. Old maids were the chief keepers of the cats.

His understanding of the relatedness of life forms once enabled Darwin to tell us something about a creature no one has ever seen, one that experts insisted did not, could not, exist. This great naturalist examined an orchid on the island of Madagascar. It secreted nectar, indicating that it was pollinated by some nectar-eating life form. The only difficulty about this reasoning was that the nectar was in the bottom of a foot-long tube extending back of the orchid. Darwin boldly predicted that a moth would be discovered on

Madagascar with a feeding tube twelve inches long! The insect experts laughed loud and long. Darwin died long before he was vindicated—but forty years after he made that ridiculous prediction, a moth was discovered on the island with a feeding tube curled under its "chin" that could be unrolled a full twelve inches. It was given the Latin name *Xanthopan morgani praedicta.*

One does not have to be a graduate ecologist to do some profitable ecological thinking. We may not come up with such amazing answers as those Darwin produced, but such thinking will at least enable us to ask the right questions. Certain insects damage fruit. Others damage or kill fruit trees. Still others destroy the leaves on fruit trees. A chemical company puts an insecticide on the market that will kill any insect that approaches the orchard. Do you want it? Not by a jugful of DDT! Without the insects to pollinate the blossoms, not one piece of fruit will be produced.

A few years ago a new fungicide was put on the market, and a magazine with a tremendous national and even worldwide circulation heralded it with an enthusiastic article. Smut on grains, it pointed out, could sometimes destroy ten percent of a crop; brown rot on stone fruits causes them to spoil as they ripen; wilts on truck crops take a tremendous toll; and all these are fungus diseases. Now mankind had a new weapon to use against these enemies, a broad-spectrum fungicide that would destroy all kinds of fungi.

The ecologist thinker will ask, "Are all fungi harmful? What are the relationships and links, other than harmful diseases, between the fungi and the crops that feed me?" Digging out the answers, he will discover a host of symbiotic relationships between wild fungi and the plants he cherishes, and many of these are vital to the crop plants. Many plant foods have to be altered by fungi before the plant can use them. The very tilth or workability of the soil depends largely on the fungi growing in it. A careless user of a powerful fungicide might find that he has cured his crops of fungus disease and killed his soil with the remedy. Besides, a fungicide that will kill all forms of fungus will keep me from enjoying many a dish of delicious wild mushrooms—and you all know how I would resent that!

Our world about us is dying for lack of ecological thinking. The area where I live once produced red clover seed as a cash crop. One could find bumblebee colonies in every fence corner. A beetle appeared that injured the leaves of clover. The "experts," mainly the county agricultural agents who thought only of immediate problems rather than overall effect, recommended the use of poisonous, broad-spectrum sprays. These sprays killed the beetles, but also killed the bumblebees that pollinated the blooms, so the clover could no longer produce viable seed. The farmers lost a cash crop and had to ship in clover seed to even produce hay.

But that is not the end of the story. The spray also killed the predator insects that were keeping the beetles under at least partial control. Further, it did not kill all of the beetles. Red clover, besides being a cultivated crop, is a thoroughly naturalized plant, growing wild by every country roadside and in every neglected piece of ground. It is impossible to seek out each wild clover plant and spray it, so a good supply of beetle breeding stock survived. As soon as rain washed the spray from the clover fields, these wild clover beetles invaded. They then had unlimited food and their enemies had been killed by sprays. Under such ideal conditions, these beetles multiply astronomically and such flashback infestations are far worse than the original ones.

What do the experts say? They never admit that they have used the wrong remedy. They recommend more and stronger sprays with even more disastrous results. The very land becomes poisonous and the rains carry this poison into the streams where it kills the fish. This not only destroys the

commercial fisherman's job and ruins the pleasure fisherman's sport, but it also interrupts other natural processes and
removes some links in vital food chains.

Fish-eating birds like the kingfisher, the osprey, and the
very symbol of America, the bald eagle, are poisoned,
rendered sterile, or starved. They could soon become extinct.
But more happens: Some small fish are very important in
mosquito control. When these are killed by sprays, the
mosquitoes proliferate and mosquito-carried diseases appear.
Do the experts trace this chain back and see that they are
responsible for the deaths that result? Not at all! They
simply recommend more, stronger, and universally distrib-
uted poisons to control the mosquitoes, thus multiplying the
disaster.

While I believe that more ecological thinking is an
absolute necessity if we are to survive and preserve an
environment that will make survival worthwhile, I don't
consider this kind of thinking an onerous task that should be
undertaken only as an alternative to disaster. Such thinking
can vastly increase your enjoyment of nature. The organic
gardeners, the organic farmers, and the organic nature lovers
are the natural ecological thinkers—and who enjoys life more
than they do? A good definition of an organic gardener is "a
gardener who thinks ecologically." The ecological approach
does not make nature study more difficult; it makes it easier.
Since ecology means the study of relationships between life
forms, it also means togetherness in nature. The study of one
life form will give information about dozens of others. When
we learn the kind of company one life form keeps, we know
what to look for whenever we encounter that plant or
animal.

24. Which Way Is Evolution Taking Nature?

WHILE visiting in Ohio I found myself seated next to a local schoolteacher at a dinner party. She was eagerly explaining to me how she was attempting to give her students a deep love of nature, when she noticed a peace symbol on my lapel. She was actually shocked and said, "How can a man who knows as much about nature as you do wear that thing? All of nature is nothing but continuous war!"

It hurts my soul to see an educated person still clinging to that ancient fallacy about the nature of nature in the last third of the twentieth century.

In the first half of the nineteenth century, when people had not observed nature closely enough to know that a barnacle was a crustacean, and that wild geese did not hatch from them, there was some excuse. Darwin and Wallace were great thinkers and among the first real observers of nature, but being beginners they were bound to fall into errors, and they did. As in other sciences, sometimes even the errors were valuable for a time, since they started others to thinking reasonably and systematically. It amazes me how few people seem to know that Darwin's theory of the "origin of the species through natural selection governed by the survival of the fittest in the struggle for existence" is not a theory accepted by the top biologists of today. Subjected to experiment it has proved fallacious and even the study of existing nature proves it does not solve the problem of the origin of the species. It does show how races, varieties, and subspecies can develop within a species, but it throws no light on how new species can come into existence.

Why, then, did the greatest minds of the nineteenth century seize onto this theory with such tenacity? I think we must look at the society in which these men lived, and largely accepted, for the answer. Anyone who has read Charles Dickens, a contemporary of these other great minds, knows that they lived in one of the most cruel, heartless, rapacious, exploitive, and repressive societies the world has ever seen. We are still dealing with some of their hangups in the areas of prejudice, prisons, mental institutions, charity hospitals, poorhouses, old folks homes, and especially in imperialistic wars. Maybe it is because we are still so close to them in our behavior that we still cling to this discredited theory. Any society must think up reasonable and logical excuses for its unreasonable and illogical actions, and what better excuse could one have than saying that such behavior is a law of nature?

Let's give the great men, Darwin and Wallace, their due. They did not say that the "fittest" was always the most violent, the most combative, the most rapacious, or the most competitive but that is the way that so-called "thinkers" of that society interpreted it. And that is the way that far too many pseudo-naturalists with a firsthand unfamiliarity with facts, still interpret what these men said—including my Ohio schoolteacher.

As these great pioneering naturalists did, I too, observe

violence and competition in nature. One would have to be blind, or close one's eyes to obvious facts, to deny that these things do exist.

But I also observe countless mercies, kindnesses, and much cooperation in nature, and I maintain that it is these that typify nature rather than the violence and competitions. My studies have gradually led me to the conclusion that it is the cooperative rather than the competitive that survives. The meek do inherit the earth.

This leads inevitably to the theory that the direction of advance in evolution is away from competition and toward cooperation. There is much evidence that this is true. The annals of paleontology are filled with the remains of predators larger and fiercer than any that exist today, and yet they are extinct. Why?

It is not only the dead species that give weight to this theory but the living ones. How did they manage to survive? Not by competitive rivalry but most often by working out a cooperative relationship with the life forms that formed their environment. There are any number of examples but we have space for only a few.

Did you ever wonder, as I have, how the flowers, which delight our eyes and nose, came into existence? This happened rather suddenly, as time is measured in an evolutionary frame of reference. A few million years ago there were plants and insects but no flowers. There is only one theory of their development that makes sense: The insects preyed on the plants, piercing their tough outsides and sucking up the sugar-bearing sap. Some plants developed tougher skins, some poisoned their sap, but some learned to follow the Biblical adage: "If thine enemy hunger, feed him." These plants put concentrated sap, or nectar, where the preying insects could get at it without inflicting injury on its generous host. Then pollen-bearing organs near these pools of nectar soon discovered that these visiting insects were so efficiently distributing the pollen that the plant could give up other methods of getting the life-bearing sperm to the right places.

Now the former freeloader was paying his board, and plants began competing for his services. They did this by competing, not by trying to destroy or injure the other plants, but by making themselves more attractive to the formerly feared and despised insects. Some tried sweeter nectar, some tried bright-colored petals to guide the insect to the dinner table, and some tried exciting perfumes to lure the insects in. The plants gained a very efficient method of pollination, the insects gained a good supply in extremely pleasant surroundings and the world gained beauty and delight. Flowers were born because nature tried peace and cooperation instead of violence and competition.

*III. Botanical
Wonders*

25. An Introduction to the World of Wildflowers

I ONCE saw a boy walk up to his father with a plant he had picked and say, "Dad, what is the name of this plant?" His father glanced at the green thing and said, "I don't know." The boy persisted: "What kind of flower does it have?" The answer again was, "I don't know." The boy then said, "But, Dad, if I were hungry, would this plant be good to eat?" Once again: "I don't know." The boy then began, "Well, what is——? *Oh*, never mind." Immediately the father became concerned, and said, "No, no, son, that's not the right attitude. Go ahead and ask questions. The only way you will ever learn anything is by asking questions."

I, too, believe in asking questions, but I want to ask them where I'll get some dependable answers. To be sure of getting good answers about wildflowers, let's ask Mother Nature some down-to-earth questions.

Why are there wildflowers? What is their function? Why does a wilderness plant produce gorgeous blooms that will never be seen by an appreciative human eye, and fill the air with a fragrant perfume that will never be enjoyed by a human nose? In what way do flowers serve the plant that produces them? Does the plant "put on" these bright colors because of a desire to be beautiful? If so, beautiful to whom or to what? What do flowers do? When we have the answers to these basic questions, we will look on a wildflower with new eyes and with a new understanding of its intricate structure.

It would seem that flowers were not intended for our enjoyment, because wildflowers existed millions of years before humans appeared. The plant does produce flowers in order to be more attractive, but we are not the ones it is trying to attract. To the plant, flowering is an essential step in the production of seed. In order to produce seeds that will grow, the pollen from the male stamens must be transported to the female pistils by some outside agent. All that beauty and fragrance, and those pools of delicious, highly flavored nectar, are produced by the plant for the creeping, crawling, and flying things that carry the pollen from flower to flower. Most flowers are meant to lure insects, but some are trying to attract nectar-eating bats—the pollen hitchhiking a ride on the bat's whiskers. Others attract nectar-eating birds—the pollen sticking to the bird's long bill. So some flowers are buggy, some are batty, and some are for the birds.

How did flowers develop? This is another good question, and even an intelligent guess at the answer will help us to understand the function and structure of every living wildflower. Once there were no flowers. For millions of years the only seedbearing plants were gymnosperms, ancestors of our present-day conifers. They depend on the wind to carry their pollen. That this method was successful is proved by the vast forests of conifers that are still around, but it was very inefficient. For every grain of pollen that made a successful boy-meets-girl rendezvous with an ovule, millions failed to make this vital contact and settled in places where their generative power was completely wasted. The number of pollen grains produced by a single pine tree is such a huge figure that it makes our national debt look like small change. I have seen forest lakes completely covered with a scum of pine pollen.

Some of these early gymnosperms had other problems. (You will remember that the conversion of water, carbon dioxide, and light into sugar by green plants is the primary industry of the whole world, and the one on which all other life depends.) One problem was that flying insects had developed, and some of them were piercing the plants with needlelike beaks, sucking dry the sugar-carrying veins. This wasn't doing the plant much good. Some plants came up with an answer to this problem: "If thine enemy be hungry, give him bread to eat." They developed little pools of concentrated sap in places where the insects could eat all the sugar they wanted, without injuring the plants. There was one catch to this free lunch. These pools of sugar syrup accumulated at the bases of the organs that produced its pollen and ovules. When an insect crawled over the pollen-producing organs to get at the sweets, pollen grains stuck to his legs by dozens. Then he flew to the ova-producing organs for the second course, and the pollen grains hopped off and started wooing the ovules. By putting these former freeloaders to work, the plant had solved both its pollen-distribution problem and its parasite problem. It had transformed its former enemies into its best friends. Now the ovules could all be fertilized without the plant having to rain pollen all over the landscape.

New problems arose. Some of these newly found best friends of the plant began eating the ovules as well as the free nectar. However, while the insects were influencing the plant to change, the plant had been altering the insects. The easy living the plants had provided for the insects had led to the insects getting soft, literally. Their hypodermic-needle beak had, in many cases, been transformed into a weak soda straw that was useful only for sucking up nectar and unprotected ovules, and could no longer pierce plant tissue. The plant had merely to put the ovules inside a fleshy vessel, which we call an ovary, and they were safe. The plant that discovered this solution became the first true angiosperm, or seed in a vessel.

This time the solution to one problem created another one. How were the pollen grains to cuddle up with the ovules when they were imprisoned in a vessel? There is an old saying, "Love will find a way," and it did, with the most fantastic invention in the whole plant kingdom—the pollen tube. The ovary grows thin stalks called styles, each topped with a sticky stigma that picks up pollen grains from the legs of any insect that happens to crawl over it on the way to the free soda fountain. As soon as it sticks to a stigma, a pollen grain starts growing a long, exceedingly thin tube down through the style and into the ovary, where it contacts an ovule and fertilizes it. This pollen tube is one of the most amazing growth phenomena in all nature. The distance from the stigma to the ovary is often several inches in large flowers, and may be as much as eighteen inches from the end of the silk to the ovules at the bottom of the ear in some varieties of corn. All this growth from a pollen grain that may be less than one-thousandth of an inch in diameter! If the pollen grain were an inch in diameter and grew a tube of proportionate length, it would reach about four miles. The pollen tube makes all that tremendous growth in a few hours.

Somewhere along the line certain plants came up with a scheme to get the pollinated insects to do twice as much work for the same pay. They just moved the stamens into the same flowers with the pistils, developing what the botanists call a perfect flower. When the insect comes for lunch, he first crawls over the stigmata, leaving pollen from another flower. Then, while he is sipping nectar, the stamens dust him with pollen from the anthers on top of the thin filaments and he carries this pollen to the next flower he visits.

As in the preceding case, the solution of one problem created a new one. When an ovule is fertilized by pollen from the same flower in which it grows, the plant loses its ability to change and adapt to new conditions as they arise. So it was desirable to have a way to insure cross-pollination. Some flowers solved this problem by growing very long styles with the stigmas towering over the much shorter filaments and anthers of the stamens. The pollinating insect, in crawling into the flower, first left pollen from another flower on the stigmas, then picked up a new load from the stamens for the next flower. Other plants never have mature pollen and mature ovules in the same flower at the same time. These failed to get the insect to do double work but they did economize on space and energy by making one flower take the place of two. Many flowers have developed ovules that are infertile to their own pollen. (That is why some kinds of fruit trees won't bear fruit unless another tree of the same kind is planted nearby to pollinate them.) There are other plants that didn't solve this problem at all, but settled for inbreeding. Such plants are usually very rigidly true to type with little or no variation, and they run the risk of being wiped out if the environment demands change, for, like some people I know, they are unchangeable.

Now let's look at the diagram of a perfect flower and see if it doesn't begin to make sense. We now know what female pistil and male stamens are all about and even how they mate. Just outside the stamens are the petals, which are collectively known as the corolla. These are nature's billboards, advertising free nectar. The pollinating insects know —by the color, shape, and size of the petals—which brand is being offered, and they head for the one that is serving the kind they like best. Outside the corolla one finds the whorl of sepals, which are collectively known as the calyx. The sepals are usually green, and when the flower is in bud these close over it and protect it until the ovules are old enough to begin considering matrimony. Often around the base of the pistil and stamens you will find the nectar, either out in the open where it can be eaten by any casual visitor, or hidden away so it can be reached by only certain specific insects which pollinate only that kind of plant.

Some wildflowers are actually as regular and orderly as the description given here, but please don't expect them all to be that way. This is the way the botany manual says they should look, but most of the wildflowers I examine seem never to have read the book. The changing and remodeling the plant had to do to produce the perfect flowers we see today did not happen in a few weeks or even in a few centuries. The daddy of Mother Nature's offspring is Father Time. It took millions of generations to achieve this perfection.

Many plants failed to make it all the way, and today we can still examine live plants in every stage between the primitive conifers and those producing perfect flowers. Some plants still produce the pollen and ovules in separate flowers on the same plant, while others even bear them on separate plants. Your English teacher might object if you wrote of a tree as "he," but some willows, poplars, and others are definitely male. You may have trouble locating the pistil, stamens, and other organs in such flowers as daisies, dandelions, and Black-eyed Susans—until you look very closely and discover that here is a really large number of individual flowers crowded together in what looks like one conspicuous bloom. On these same flowers you can see another example of cooperation and division of labor in nature. The outer flowers on many kinds of these composite blooms can no longer bear seed. Their task is to grow the colored, straplike petals that surround the bloom in order to attract pollinating insects so their neighbors can develop seeds capable of

germination. You will find many other such strange varia-
tions and adaptations which will help you realize that,
however slowly, nature is forever in a state of change and
development.

I love wildflowers. If I am camping when the fragrant
white clusters of black locust blooms cover the trees, I gather
a few of these grapelike clusters, make a fritter batter of some
biscuit mix, milk, an egg, and some sugar; dip each cluster in
the batter; then fry them in deep fat. They are delicious. The
clusters of elderberry blooms can be fried in the same way, as
can the large orange-colored blooms of the daylilies that
grow by so many roadsides. Sometimes I don't even let the
daylilies bloom, but pick off the unopened buds and cook
and serve them exactly as I would green beans. A notable
vegetable. Eating flowers really shouldn't seem strange to us.
Cauliflower and broccoli are both flower buds of the plants
that bear them.

You probably have eaten a part of a flower quite recently.
Have you eaten a peach, a plum, a cherry, or most any other
fruit? Remember those fleshy vessels the flower developed to
protect the ovules? Well, much of the fruit that you eat is
this ovary, grown large and matured. How did the plant
develop that little protective ovary into the sweet, luscious
fruits that we all enjoy? While we can only surmise the
answer, that very conjecture will help us to understand the
wildflower and its function and structure.

We have seen how plants solved the problems of pollination so they could produce seed that would grow. But they
still had problems. One was that seeds tended to fall straight
down from where they were ripened, and crowd on one
another, trying to grow right under the parent plant. How
much better it would be if the plant could invent some way
to send its seed on a journey where it could pick out a new
location. Different plants have solved this problem in many

different ways. Some—the cottonwoods and milkweeds are good examples—grew very lightweight seed with streamers of silk attached to them, so the wind would carry them off and scatter them far and wide. Others, and here the maple and the ash are examples, grew wings on the ovary that enclosed the seed; then, when the ripened fruit dropped, it went whirling off like a helicopter. Still others, such as the wild touch-me-not, often called the jewelweed, and the witch hazel went in for artillery. They developed the ovary into a seedpod, which would break open with explosive force when the seeds were ripe, throwing them many feet from the plant. Others—and here some examples are beggar-ticks, cockle-burs, cleavers, and burdock—grew spines or sticky bristles on the ovary, and, when the seed was ripe, these would steal a ride in the fur of a passing animal.

But there were other plants and quite a few of them, that developed the inspired solution, "Love your enemies; win over those that are harming you and make them into helpers." One could almost say that nature remembered how it had changed parasites into pollen carriers and decided to try something in that line again. Mammals and birds had developed, and some of them were a nuisance. They were eating leaves and roots to get the little sugar they had in them. A plant happened to build an ovary out of plant tissue compounds that became sweet as the seed ripened. An animal took this fruit and ate it, dropping the seeds in a new place. Now the race was on. The plant that produced the sweetest and best fruit would attract the most animals, which would scatter its seeds the farthest, so the very best wild fruits became most widely scattered and most often survived to produce others of its kind.

Now we can answer that question about why plants developed delicious fruits. They grow those fruits as a free gift to passing animals, even if some of those animals happen to be wearing Boy Scout uniforms. The animals, in turn, unconsciously scatter the seeds of the plants. So when you stop to eat wild cherries, blueberries, or ripe persimmons while on a hike, you are playing the role nature intended you to play. Get out to the fields and woods—there is a world of fascinating nature lore as well as some mighty fine food waiting for you.

26. How to Milk
a Milkweed

THE milkweed's biggest handicap is its second syllable. A weed, by definition, is a plant that we don't like and don't want around. It's an epithet of prejudice. But get really acquainted with this wondrous plant and you might find yourself thinking of it instead as the "milkplant," "milkflower," or maybe even reverently and liturgically as *Asclepias syriaca*, its euphonious Latin name. If you live west of a line extending straight north from eastern Texas through Minnesota and into southern Canada, you can formally address their similar species as *Asclepias speciosa*, an even more elaborate appellation for so humble a wild plant. This name, as translated, means "the showy flower of Aesculapias," the Greek God of medicine.

The milkweed, so familiar, even unavoidable over its vast domain, scarcely needs describing. But those who've never crossed a vacant lot nor looked out a car window at the roadside vegetation can recognize this plant by its stout, unbranched stalk, three- to five-feet tall at maturity, clothed in pairs of thick, dark green, oblong leaves, four to eight inches long and about half as broad; and by clusters of very fragrant flowers, whitish-rose to purple in color in both species, followed by large, warty seedpods filled with silk, and finally by thick, milky sap. Some very unwholesome plants have sap that is identical in appearance, prompting the admonitions that you can't identify milkweed by its sap alone.

This "weed" is versatile in more ways than you will believe. The young shoots can be gathered in late spring when they are from four to eight inches high. Rub the natal wool off them, then cook and serve like asparagus. But they don't taste like asparagus and a great many people propose that they're better.

If you get there too late for the shoots, don't despair. Gather the tender, young, top leaves and prepare them like spinach. Loaded with vitamins C and A, they taste good if properly prepared and seasoned. You can use a bit of the young leaf in a salad, but don't overdo it. Raw milkweed leaves should be considered salad herbs, not salad vegetables. Their primary function is as flavoring, not substance.

When the flower buds that appear in the axils of upper leaves become grayish-green hemispheres an inch or so across, composed of crowded, beadlike buds, they can be gathered and cooked in the same manner as broccoli. This is my favorite milkweed vegetable, and I like it so well that I not only eat it in season but blanch and freeze enough for winter.

Finally, when the warty pods are only two inches long, firm in texture, and the silk and seeds are still undeveloped, they can be gathered and cooked like okra. At this stage the insides of the pods cook up into a soft mass that is delicious and nourishing. If you find that the silk is noticeable, you have pods that are too old.

So much for the wonders of milkweed. Now for the

drawbacks. All four of these milkweed vegetables are bitter—
so bitter that few people can enjoy them unprocessed. I
freely admit that I am not numbered among those who like
them with all their native, excruciatingly bitter flavor.
Fortunately, the processing to tame that bitterness down to
palatable levels is easily done. Whatever you do, don't put
milkweed vegetables into cold water and then heat them.
Apparently the bitter principle is located mainly in the
outermost cellular layers, those exposed to the sunlight.
Heating the cold vegetable gradually drives this bitterness
inward and distributes it throughout the food. Instead, put
the washed vegetable into a cooking pot, then pour boiling
water over it. Heat only until this water regains a boil, then
pour that water off. If you want a very mild vegetable, repeat
this process one or two times, then cook until tender. Season
with salt, pepper, and butter. Serve proudly.

I can already hear the protests of a thousand health food
cooks, "Doesn't all that boiling and draining destroy the
vitamins?" "No," I insist, "it doesn't." With the help of the
Food and Nutrition Department of the Penn State University, I have thoroughly explored this question. Granted that
blanching the vegetables in water that is already boiling does
leach out about twenty-five percent of the vitamin C; but it
protects the remainder and seemingly doesn't affect the
vitamin A, which is not water soluble. Vitamin C is destroyed
at an alarming rate by merely exposing the picked vegetable
to air. Milkweed vegetables processed in boiling water a few
minutes after they are picked will have far more vitamins
than the finest vegetable picked last week, displayed on the
produce shelf for two days, then stored in your refrigerator
two days more before they are cooked. Any attempt to cook
such vegetables in a manner to conserve their vitamin
content is an effort to save something that is already lost.
The only people who are getting all the vitamins nature

intended them to get from green vegetables are those who eat them freshly plucked from their own organic gardens or freshly gathered from nature's organic garden, the wild.

Pouring boiling water over milkweed buds or pods brings another glad surprise. Both these products are grayish-green in color, somewhat fuzzy, and, in short, unappealing to the eye. But bring on the boiling water and they turn a beautiful emerald green to rival in appearance anything stocked on the produce shelves. Properly processed, cooked, and seasoned, they will rival anything in flavor, too.

The American Indians knew another secret of the milkweed. All the milkweed vegetables contain some meat-tenderizing properties. When the only meat available was the tough flesh of some ancient buffalo bull, the Indians boiled up a stew with milkweed pods and made the meat as tender as baby beef. Try it—it really works.

The bark or rind of the stout milkweed stem contains a very strong fiber, as rugged as good twine. You can strip off a string of this to tie a bundle of vegetables. Or, with just a little skill, you can make your own twine. A friend of mine once showed me how he could contrive fishing gear from the wild. He stripped off a handful of this fiber-bearing bark, rubbed it between his hands and washed it at the lakeside to remove all the nonfibrous material. He then spun the pure fiber into a strong, thin line by rolling it on his thigh with the palm of his hand, in the same way that primitive peoples have spun fibers since time immemorial. His next step was to cut a slender rod from a lean willow and fasten it to a milkweed line as long as the rod. On the free end of the line he fastened a thorn from a hawthorn bush that had been sharpened until the butt end was as sharp as the thorn end, and then he cut a shallow groove in the middle to hold the line. He found an earthworm under a rock for bait and, holding one end of the double-ended thorn against the line, he slid the worm over the thorn—line and all. This was tossed out and as it slowly sank into the lake a greedy bluegill came up and swallowed the whole worm. A pull turned the thorn crosswise in the fish's gullet and he was snared but good. One hour after my friend started stripping the fiber from a milkweed plant he had more little six-inch bluegills than both of us could eat at one meal. We ate them with boiled milkweed pods and fared very well, thank you.

This line could also be knotted into fishnets, or a number of smaller lines could be twisted together to make a strong rope. It could be netted into a carrying bag or even woven into a coarse cloth, although I doubt that milkweed cloth— rough on the skin as it is—will ever make it big on the textile scene.

Another interesting milkweed product is the silk found in the mature pods. It's that super-light, spangled fluff attached to each seed that actually enables it to fly. Strike a dry, open milkweed pod and watch how many of these parachuted seeds drift, not downard, but upward, to sail off and start new milkweed patches in other locations. Imagine how light this fluff of milkweed down would be without the weight of the clinging seed! I'm not exactly the Eli Whitney of the milkweed pod, but I have discovered a fairly easy way to collect the pure down. If you pluck the pod when fully mature and open it carefully, you will see before you a beautiful arrangement. The silk lies smoothly along the central core, covered by seeds arranged as carefully as the scales on a fish. If you grasp the upper, pointed end of the removed silk spool, you can scrape off a ring of seeds with your thumbnail. Move your fingers down gradually scraping off more and more seeds until the last ones are gone. The pure silk can then be rubbed off into a box, barrel, or bag. Be sure you confine it or it will just float away as soon as it unfolds. Due to its shape and lightness I've found that a very few pods fill quite a large box to overflowing, and that the whole boxful probably weighs less than an ounce. After drying the fluff, press it down, and add another ounce. Repeating this process a few times, you can get several ounces into a good-sized box.

During World War II our government tried using this silk as a substitute for kapok in filling life preservers. This was like making potato bags of pure silk. They simply were not asking enough of this wonderful fluff. I would like to try it as a substitute for goosedown in insulating sleeping bags and garments for use in the Arctic. In a catalog before me prime Northern goosedown is priced at well over one dollar per ounce. I wonder if milkweed fluff wouldn't actually do a better job, and at those prices I could certainly find someone to gather it. I have a great cardboard drum filled with the stuff right now and I intend to fill a camp pillow with it to see how it stands up to use.

Now, about the milk inside this plant: It looks like thick cream but don't imagine you can eat it on a dish of wild fruit. It is a latex from which perfectly good rubber could be refined, hardly a task you could undertake out in camp or even at home. No matter, you can use it unrefined in several ways. First, it is an eminently available, efficient, and easy-to-use multipurpose glue, strong enough to fasten an emergency patch on a tent or poncho.

I have seen Indian children in New Mexico and children in Indiana use this latex for chewing gum. They break the latex veins in the middle of the large leaf exposed to the sun and, when the rubbery stuff has dried sufficiently, they chew it. I've tried it myself and, believe me, you have to persevere. It tastes very bitter at first but this soon changes and it becomes at least bearable. The fact that these children chew it throughout the time it's in season shows that a real taste for it can be acquired. Finally, this milky sap is reputed to be a cure for warts, to be rubbed on the wart every day until it disappears.

I have read at least six reports that a good brown sugar can be made from milkweed blossoms, but all of these reports show evidence of coming from the same source. Directions are given to gather the flowers when heavily covered with dew, squeeze out this dew, and boil it down like maple sap. I tried this, feeling like a fool (a very appropriate feeling in this case!) for I knew that this dew was no more than atmospheric moisture condensed on the flowers and couldn't possibly contain sugar. It didn't. I might as well have boiled tap water.

But milkweed flowers do contain large amounts of sweet nectar. Beekeepers in areas where this plant is abundant speak of the "milkweed flow" as a source of honey. I reasoned that maybe I could wash this nectar out in cold water, boil it down, and make sugar. I gathered half a bushel of flower clusters and washed them all, a few at a time, in about two quarts of water. Then I strained out the insects that had been dislodged in this process and boiled down this presumably nectar-rich solution. I got a couple of table-spoons of a dark syrup. It must have been mostly sugar but was so bitter that I could hardly taste the sweetness. Until some reader advises me of a better way to extract this sugar, I'll leave the task to the bees and eat their finished product.

Surely a plant that can furnish four different vegetables, fishlines, nets, and ropes, an insulating material of unparalleled softness and lightness, a good glue, chewing gum, a cure for warts, and good honey doesn't have to produce still another product to win our love.

27. The World of Conifers

T HEY stand tall among the popular symbols of the holiday season. Green, graceful, and gayly decorated, these Yuletide members-of-the-family share top billing with Santa, snow, and sleighs. Although you probably have one—big or small—in your home each year, how much do you know about the ever-present evergreens called conifers?

Anyone who can tell a tree from a telephone pole can usually distinguish a conifer, such as a pine, spruce, fir, or hemlock, from a broad-leaved tree, such as an oak, beech, hickory, or cottonwood. But it is not easy to define a conifer in simple terms. Ask a tree-smart friend for a precise definition of coniferous trees and the chances are you can pick holes in his answer. Coniferous means "cone-bearing," but such undisputed conifers as yews and junipers bear their seed in what looks suspiciously like a berry Most conifers have needlelike foliage, but it takes a powerful imagination to see anything needlelike in the flat foliage of a conifer such as the agathis of the Southern Hemisphere. Lumbermen call conifers "softwoods" and broad-leaved trees "hardwoods," yet the wood of such a softwood as longleaf yellow pine is far harder than that of such hardwoods as basswood, poplar, or cottonwood.

Most conifers are evergreens, but so are such broad-leaved trees as holly and live oak, while a few conifers—the larch and the bald cypress are examples—shed their needles every fall and grow a new crop in the spring.

If your tree-trained friend says that conifers are gymnosperms, while broad-leaved trees are angiosperms, he knows what he's talking about. These sound like five-dollar words, but they are worth learning—they represent a very real meaningful division in the plant kingdom. All living seed-bearing plants are either gymnosperms or angiosperms. Gymnosperm means "naked seed," and angiosperm means "seed in a vessel."

In reproduction the gymnosperms, including all conifers, bear naked ovules in seed cones that are fertilized by direct landing of a grain of windblown pollen from the male pollen cones. This occurs by accident but is not as chancey as it might seem, for the male pollen cones of the conifers produce unbelievable amounts of pollen. Strike a branch of a pine tree during pollen time and you will see what I mean: The air will fill with millions of pollen grains, and each ovule is almost certain to receive its grain of pollen.

Even with these two handy terms, the definition of "conifer" is still likely to get a bit hazy around the edges, because, while all conifers are gymnosperms, not all gymnosperms are conifers. However, all native, tree-sized gymnosperms in temperate North America are conifers. The ginkgo, a very interesting gymnosperm with foliage resembling an overgrown maidenhair fern, is often planted as an ornamental in the United States; but it is not a native, having been naturalized from Asia. Practically speaking, there is no difficulty whatever in recognizing the conifers. Their characteristic foliage and growth habits, as well as their often majestic size and great beauty, make the mighty conifers unmistakable.

The conifers are often called "living fossils" because they appeared on the earth many millions of years before the first angiosperm developed a flower with petals, stamens, and pistil. The conifers' simple reproductive system, with its naked ovules and windblown pollen, has been called primitive. This is not fair. True, the most sophisticated angiosperms bear more beautiful flowers and may enlist the aid of flying insects to transport the male pollen to the female ovule (and thus can produce less pollen because it is used more efficiently). But this doesn't prove that the conifers are inferior. The conifers couldn't use this modern, airmail delivery of pollen because they had to solve the problem long before the first flying insect took wing. Judging from the number of conifers still around, I would say they worked out a pretty good solution.

Conifers may be primitive, in the sense that they arrived on the scene in very early times, but they certainly are not crude. Not only have they persisted in competition with later vegetation, they have proved superbly adaptable. Today conifers grow around the world, in both the Northern and Southern hemispheres. In the United States, some species reach beyond the Arctic Circle in Alaska, while others grow in the subtropical Florida Keys. They grow mighty forests from the rockbound coast of Maine to Southern California. Some become soaring giants in the rain forests of the Pacific Northwest, while others beautify the arid hills of Arizona. Conifers rule the mountains, foresting the middle slopes with mighty trees and then developing smaller, high-altitude species that push the timberline up thousands of feet. Other species grow in brackish swamps at sea level. The largest living thing is a conifer. The tallest thing alive is a conifer. The tallest tree measured was recently discovered in California, a coast redwood that stands 367.8 feet high. The largest thing alive is probably the famous General Sherman tree, in Sequoia National Park. This giant sequoia measures 101.5 feet around the base, with a mean diameter of thirty-two feet at the base. At 100 feet above the ground it still measures eighteen feet in diameter, and the largest limb, 130 feet above the ground, is 6.5 feet in diameter. The total weight of this giant is estimated to be 2150 tons, and it could yield enough lumber to build a good-sized village. This tree is estimated to be about 3,000 years old. It was already a huge tree when Julius Caesar's legions were conquering Gaul. It was once thought to be the oldest living thing, but some recent ring-counting on the bristlecone pine has shown that the General Sherman is a mere youngster in comparison to these ancient mountain-dwellers. One bristlecone pine has been found to be 4,600 years old. There is something awe-inspiring in a tree that has been alive throughout all of recorded history.

We should realize, when talking of "the oldest living thing," that the age of a tree is not strictly comparable to the age of an animal. An animal must stay alive all over and all the way to the very center of his body, in order to stay alive at all; but nine-tenths of the mighty bulk of the General Sherman tree is unliving heartwood, made up of long-dead cells. Only a comparatively thin outer layer of this majestic tree is actually alive. It is doubtful if a single living cell of the General Sherman was alive thirty years ago. Most animals achieve maturity and then stop growing; a tree must keep growing in order to stay alive.

Most people are under the impression that a tree is fed by its roots. Even the poet, Joyce Kilmer, writes of "A tree whose hungry mouth is pressed/ Against the Earth's sweet flowing breast." If this "sweet flowing breast" was the tree's only source of food, it would soon starve to death. But, as I have explained, the roots don't feed the tree; they give it water in which minerals are dissolved, so these so-called plant foods are not food at all in the sense that they can be used as energy or add to the tree's growth. The dissolved minerals furnished by the roots are raw materials for the tree's food factories, which are the leaves, or, in the case of the conifers, the needles. A tree lives on sugar, and this sugar is manufactured not by the roots but by the leaves.

I don't know why so many botanical writers persist in downgrading the pine needle in comparison to the broad leaves of the deciduous trees. One writes, "unlike the advanced flowering trees which have evolved broad leaves with profusely branching veins, the most primitive conifers have never gone beyond their simple cluster of needles." Why should they? I'm not so sure that those broad but shortlived leaves are an "advance" over pine needles. Broad leaves are not very durable, and must often be replaced every year, while the pine needle may continue to make sugar at full capacity for five years or so before it needs replacement. Pines do shed their needles, as anyone knows who has ever unrolled his sleeping bag on a soft, springy, fragrant bed of them. But the pine wisely grows a replacement needle before the old one wears out, so the tree is continuously in full foliage.

While the needle of a white pine may appear to be a very simple thing, a cross-section of it viewed under a powerful microscope reveals that it is very complex and highly organized. The cross-section is roughly triangular in shape, with a single vein down the center. The vein contains tubes that distribute the water and minerals coming from the roots, and other tubes that transport the dissolved sugar made by the needle to any other part of the tree that needs food.

Outside the vein are the sugar-producing cells, and out near the covering are the resin ducts. The resin ducts are the maintenance engineers of this sugar factory. Any wound, leak, or scratch in the needle is promptly patched with resin

white pine

(*Pinus Strobus*)

until cell growth can make a permanent repair. The resin probably also serves as an antifreeze to keep the needle pliable and operative in cold weather, despite its high water content. All of this wonderful mechanism is protected by a hard covering dotted with hundreds of tiny openings that adjust automatically to regulate air intake according to the cells' needs.

Some of the greatest accomplishments of space-age technology have been in the field of miniaturization, reducing bulky and heavy mechanisms to such small size and light weight that they can be carried on our space vehicles. However, man still has a long way to go to equal what the pine tree accomplished in this field many millions of years ago. The complete sugar factory described above is confined in a needle only a few inches long, about one-sixteenth of an inch in diameter, and weighing a small fraction of an ounce. These small, compact, thick-walled needles are well adapted to a variety of climates and weather, and they enable the conifer to keep its food factories operating the year around, from the Arctic to the tropics.

A sugar molecule contains atoms of hydrogen, oxygen, and carbon. The pine needles use hydrogen from water furnished by the tree roots, and carbon and oxygen from the carbon dioxide in the air breathed in by those adjustable pores on the needle's surface. It takes tremendous amounts of energy to tear the carbon dioxide molecule apart and recombine it with water to form a sugar molecule, so this sugar factory must have a power source. That source is the most primary and powerful of all sources: the sun. The magic chlorophyll in the food-producing cells has the ability to transform light energy into chemical energy. This is the most basic of all basic industries in this world, for all other earthly life depends on this transformation of water and carbon dioxide into sugar. As an added service it removes excess carbon dioxide from the atmosphere and increases the supply of available oxygen, thus keeping our air breathable.

Economically, conifers are far more important than deciduous hardwoods. About four-fifths of all lumber produced in the United States comes from conifers. Nearly all of the paper manufactured in this country is made of conifer pulpwood. Millions of young conifers, sold as Christmas trees, have rejuvenated many thousands of square miles of submarginal farmland. Hundreds of thousands of young conifers are sold each year to be planted as ornamentals, adding to the beauty of our cities, parks, and roadsides. Commercial turpentine, pine tar, and resin all originate in the resin ducts of conifers.

It was the conifers that gave America the chewing-gum habit. Long before the arrival of the white man, Indians were chewing spruce gum and the hardened, fragment resin of the balsam fir. In the West, the Indians chewed the hardened resin of the piñon or nut pine. I probably chewed several tons of piñon gum during my boyhood in New Mexico. Like spruce gum, it is found on the tree in hard translucent golden nuggets, but it turns pink between the teeth. It was only when some clever businessman saw how devotedly children were chewing these natural gums that commercial chewing gum appeared on the market.

Fluffy lumps of almost pure sugar gum are found on the giant sugar pines of California and Oregon, where these trees have been injured. To a lost hunter it could furnish nourishing food and the energy to walk back to civilization.

Pine needles are rich in vitamin C. In the days before the invention of artificial refrigeration and modern canning methods, nearly everyone lived during the winter on salted or dried food. In late winter many of these people suffered, and some died, from scurvy, which is caused by vitamin C deficiency. Vitamin C is water soluble, and pine needle tea could have prevented these deaths, had the people only known to use it. It isn't a bad drink either; try it on your next camping trip. Just put a handful of pine needles in a teapot and fill the pot with boiling water. Let them steep awhile, add sugar, then drink the tea.

The Indians often ate the immature male pollen cones, the tender new growth, and the inner bark of several of the pines. All these pine products were boiled with meat, if it was available, or alone, if it wasn't. They make excellent survival food, being rich in sugar and starch. The Shakers of New England used to sell the candied new growth of white pine. These shoots were peeled, boiled until tender, then boiled in strong sugar syrup. I find them delicious, but some of my friends object to the "piny" taste.

The most delicious pine product is the nut produced by several species of pine. The ancient Romans appreciated these delicacies, and they are still eaten in the Old World, from Italy to Siberia. Western America is very well supplied with the nut-bearing pines. When I was a boy in New Mexico I often gathered piñon nuts by stealing them from the nests of pack rats. This may have been a dirty trick, but I noticed that the pack rats never became scarcer because of my depredations. They continued to be pests. One could often find several quarts of piñon nuts in one pack rat nest. The nuts were delicious to eat, either raw or roasted, and they brought a good price on the market.

Many other Western pines produce edible nuts, including the wide-ranging Ponderosa pine and that mighty giant, the sugar pine, which sometimes bears cones eighteen-inches long by four inches in diameter, filled with edible nuts. The largest cones of all are produced by the Coulter pine and the digger pine, both of California. These enormous cones are often a foot long and half a foot in diameter, weighing more than four pounds apiece. Both have enormous cones filled with edible nuts, as does the rare Torrey pine, which has the most limited range of any pine, being found only on an eight-mile-long strip of the California coast and on Santa Barbara Island.

Conifers are wonderful trees, and well worth the effort it takes to get better acquainted with them.

28. An Introduction to the World of Broad-Leaved Trees

ONE DAY my grandson and I were picking up the nuts under the black walnut tree that grows in my backyard. He gazed up into the branches overhead and asked, "Grandpa, how high is this tree?" I backed off, tried to judge how many times my own height of six feet the tree extended upward to make what my grandson calls "one of Grandpa's guesstimates," and told him it was over fifty but less than sixty feet tall.

That afternoon he invaded my study, carrying a yardstick and wearing a smug grin. He said, "Grandpa, that walnut tree is only forty-six and one-half feet tall." I asked him how he had managed to measure its height with a yardstick and he answered, "It was easy, I stuck a stick in the ground and cut it off at just three feet high. Then I measured the shadow of the stick. It was just 2 feet 7½ inches when I first measured it, but it was getting longer all the time. I waited until the shadow was just three feet long. Then I knew that the shadow of the tree was just as long as the tree was high, so I measured the shadow."

I was flabbergasted. In all my long love affair with nature it had never occurred to me to determine a tree's height by this method. I went out with him to see if I could regain some of my lost prestige. The shadow of the stick was now nearly four-feet long. I asked him how he would solve the problem this late in the afternoon and he quickly answered that he would wait until the shadow of the three-foot stick was just six feet long, then measure the shadow of the tree and divide its length by two. This wasn't exactly what I had in mind. I asked him what he would do if I demanded the answer right now, without waiting on any shadows. He said he would ask me what was my hurry. This wasn't what I had in mind either.

I measured the shadow of the stick and found it to be just 3 feet 11 inches long. To make my problem easier to explain I waited until the shadow was exactly four feet long. I had to endure a sarcastic question about "Who's waiting for shadows now?" but I ignored this. When the shadow was exactly four feet long I explained that now every four feet of the tree's shadow equaled three feet of the tree's height, or that the tree was three-fourths as tall as its shadow was long. We measured and found the tree's shadow just sixty-two feet long: $\frac{3}{4} \times 62 = 46\frac{1}{2}$. My grandson informed me that he had already told me the height of the tree.

However, he was interested in this extension of his method. He scratched his head and thought awhile, then announced that he could use this shadow method to measure the height of any tree, any time the sun was shining, and that he wouldn't need to measure either the stick's shadow or the tree's shadow in feet and inches, and he wouldn't have to wait even one minute for the shadow to become a certain length. All he needed to know was the height of the stick.

This I wanted to see. He cut a thin switch, laid it along the shadow of the stick, and cut it the same length as the shadow. He then proudly explained that right at that moment each length of this switch on the shadow of the tree represented three feet on the height of the tree. He then measured the shadow of the tree with his switch and found it to be just 15½ switch-lengths long: 15½ × 3 = 46½. I decided to give up this shadowboxing game. The kid had me bested.

I next asked him how he would find the height of this tree on a cloudy day, and this time I had him where it hurts. He couldn't think of any way to do this. I put the yardstick straight up and down on the trunk of the tree and made chalk marks just three feet apart on the bark. Then I had him hold the yardstick at arm's length and back away from the tree until the two marks appeared to be just an inch apart on the yardstick. Then he was to line the zero end of the yardstick with the tip-top of the tree and slide his thumb down the yardstick until it was exactly lined with the base of the tree. Every inch of the distance between his thumb and the upper end of the yardstick then represented three feet in the tree's height. He tried it, and it came out 15½ inches, as nearly as makes no difference: 15½ × 3 = 46½. By this time we were both ready to concede that the tree was really 46½ feet tall.

I then showed him how to determine the diameter of the tree. Tree diameter is usually taken breast-high to a tall lumberjack, or at about 4½ feet above the base. Using a cloth tapemeasure, we measured around the tree at this height and found it was 51 inches in circumference. We divided this by 3, giving us 17 inches as the diameter of the tree. Yes, I know it's really supposed to be 3.14159265 + or some such ungodly number, but tree circumferences are seldom perfect circles, so just a plain three gives a pretty good average diameter and is a lot easier to divide by.

My grandson began carrying a tapemeasure and a yardstick wherever he went and during the next few days he measured the heights and diameters of nearly every tree in the neighborhood and reported the results back to me. I began feeling like the boy whose teacher gave him a book on trees as a reading assignment; the boy started his book report by writing, "This book taught me a lot more about trees than I wanted to know."

Despite being bored to tears by the height and diameters of trees, I was careful not to discourage the boy in this new pursuit, for he was painlessly acquiring valuable new knowledge. Each tree he measured was looked up in his tree guide, and he delighted in finding trees taller than the maximum height given in the book for that species. All of us like to prove the experts wrong.

Most of the trees my grandson is so industriously measuring belong to that group commonly called the broad-leaved trees, deciduous trees, or hardwoods. These are all inexact names, for a few of these trees have leaves so narrow they almost resemble conifer needles, others are not deciduous at all but evergreen, keeping their leaves over winter, and some of these so-called hardwoods have woods far softer than that of many conifers. They usually have broad leaves that fall off in the winter and are renewed every spring and they often yield hard and beautiful woods prized by cabinetmakers.

Instead of bearing pollen cones and seed cones like the conifers, the angiosperms usually have true flowers, and instead of depending on the wind to scatter their pollen, as the conifers do in hopes that some will land on the naked seeds, the angiosperms often trade some sweet nectar to insects in exchange for airmail delivery of their pollen directly to the place where it is needed. One of the most important differences between these two groups, and the one which gave them their names, is that the angiosperms enclose the female ova in a fleshy vessel instead of leaving them naked on cone scales as the gymnosperms do. This fleshy vessel, called an ovary, often develops into a fruit; so all our fruit trees, both wild and tame, are angiosperms.

The angiosperms are latecomers on the scene, compared to the extremely ancient conifers. However, the angiosperms proved to be more efficient, and they began pushing the conifers out of all the most desirable places, until today the conifers have been largely banished to the mountains, the far North, and into poor, sandy locations. Not all angiosperms are trees, for this group includes all flowering plants, from the tiny bluets in the grass to the giant magnolia.

If my grandson wants to continue to measure these broadleaved trees, he is not likely to run out of new material to work on, for there are about 150,000 different species of angiosperm trees, while there are a mere 450 species of coniferous trees. When the first white men came to America, it was one vast forest of broad-leaved, deciduous trees from the Eastern Seaboard to the Great Plains. A squirrel could have crossed Pennsylvania in any direction without ever coming to the ground. Today, it is hard to realize the important role that this tremendous forest played in our early history, and how tree-wise the early settlers had to be.

Imagine that you live in the times when the population of America was concentrated in a narrow strip along the Atlantic. You are adventurous, with a yearning to help tame the great wilderness to the West. You marry the girl of your dreams, load her in your covered wagon, and head across the Alleghenies. You reach the frontier of civilization, and a few miles beyond the last settler's cabin you come on a tract of fine, level land with deep, dark-colored, easily worked soil. The very density and size of the mighty hardwood trees that cover the ground show that the soil is fertile and productive. There is a quiet brook that will furnish water for your livestock and a cold spring that will furnish your own drinking water and refrigeration. You decide to homestead this choice site.

In order to turn this virgin forest into a productive farm and a comfortable home, you simply must know a great deal about trees. You must know which species will furnish durable, straight, and easily hewed logs from which you can build your cabin, and which tree has straight-grained wood that will easily split into homemade shingles for your roof. You need to know, too, which ones have interwoven grain and will not split, for from these you will carve the bread tray on which your wife will mix dough, and the bread board and rolling pin with which she will prepare it for the oven. Then you will have to know which furnish firewood that will burn long and hot, so she can bake the dough.

In clearing your field you must know which trees can be easily killed by merely girdling them with shallow ax cuts and which must be chopped down, which ones will die and which ones will sprout back. You must also know which trees to leave unharmed. That oak grove will furnish tons of acorns on which your pigs can fatten for your winter's meat. That stand of maples will become your sugar bush, providing you with the finest sugar and syrup ever eaten. Those shell-bark hickories, black walnuts, and butternuts will yield bushels of delicious nuts to supplement your scanty rations. The persimmons, pawpaws, wild mulberries, shadberries, and wild cherries will be your only source of fruit until you can bring an orchard into production.

In order to stay alive you must know which wood will make an ox yoke, so you can farm your land and raise your food; which wood can be used to replace a broken gunstock, so you can kill game for meat and protect your family from Indian raids; which wood will bend perfectly to make a spinning wheel; which you will use in constructing a loom; and what altogether different kind of wood will make the best loom shuttle, so your wife can weave the homespun clothes and bedcovers that protect you from the cold. A baby is born, and you must know which wood can be fashioned into a rocker for a cradle; someone dies, and you must know which tree furnishes the best lumber for a coffin.

How did the early pioneer distinguish between the many different kinds of trees, and tell one from another? They would have laughed at that question. How do you tell your mother from her sister? They have the same number of arms and legs and only one head apiece. Their bodily curves probably protrude and recede in approximately the same areas. Most likely their complexions are somewhat alike, and there may be a fairly close family resemblance, but you are never in the slightest doubt about which is your aunt.

The early settlers knew the trees in the same way and for the same reasons: they were so familiar with the trees that they automatically recognized them on sight. They probably used many clues and minor differences to distinguish between them, just as you do to tell the difference between your mother and your aunt, but both you and they were totally unconscious of using them.

The good news is that you can learn to recognize the trees in the same offhand manner the pioneers used. I know because I can now recognize several hundred different kinds of trees without ever stopping to think how I know them. It doesn't take a lifetime to do this. My grandson, who is just graduating from the Cub Scouts, knows almost as many trees as I do, and he is not aware that he ever put out much effort in studying trees. He makes friends with them, gets acquainted with them, and relates to them.

Being my grandson, he early developed a taste for wild fruits and nuts. He soon knew every tree that could furnish him with something good to eat. His face was often purple from mulberries or sticky from ripe persimmons. His mother claims she has learned to recognize many trees from the remains of their products that she finds on his face. He soon learned to distinguish between the sweet shell-bark hickory nut and the inedible bitternut, by the leaves and bark of the trees that bore them. This led to an interest in tree leaves, and he soon had a large leaf collection and could talk learnedly about compound and simple leaves, serrations, lobes, veins, and stipules, or leaf stalks.

When we made maple sugar in the early spring he found that he could tell trees apart even when they had no leaves, by their winter buds and by their bark. For awhile he took pictures of bark, and I had to sit through many slide shows trying to identify the trees by the pictures of the bark. His greatest joy was to catch me in a mistake, for his main hobby, as we have seen, is confounding the experts.

If you want to know the trees, don't study them, but get out and do something with them that is fun. Make wild fruit trees and wild nut trees furnish some of your food when you're out on a hike. Learn to tap maples and birches for their sweet sap, and learn to boil it down to make syrup for your camp flapjacks. Make collections of leaves, winter buds, or photos of bark textures. Above all, look at them, become acquainted with them and make friends with them, and then you will find that you can recognize them at a glance, just as you do your other friends.

29. Three Plants

THE pre-Columbian Indians of the United States, from Canada southward and from the Great Basin eastward, were all more or less agricultural. Their chief crops, corn, squash, and beans, were called "the three sisters." Corn and the squashes will not survive in the wild, nor will the domesticated varieties of beans, even though they have some close wild relatives. To enjoy these three fine food plants, the Indians had to grow them.

However, their plant food diet was far from being limited to these three plants. Their approach to agriculture was so different from ours that we find their viewpoint hard to grasp. They did not draw the clear line between domesticated and undomesticated plants that we do between crops and weeds. Even in their fields and gardens they not only allowed but actually encouraged certain volunteer wild food plants to grow, and harvested and used them with the same care that they rendered the planted crops. Caring and harvesting did not stop at the edge of the field. Natural wild growths of food plants were encouraged, protected, and often actually owned by individuals or families, and were marked by tying certain other plants to them. Other Indians generally respected these ownership marks.

The encouragement given to wild food plants ranged from merely pulling out or chopping down competing vegetation, through pruning (especially with wild grapes), to burning off brush and forests, so that blueberries, raspberries, fireweed, and other wild food plants could take over. Being agriculturalists, they understood seeds and planting and knew about transplanting. Using these methods they were able to induce many wild food plants to grow at convenient locations. Some were planted in gardens or vineyards and grown in rows. The Indians also moved wild food plants from areas where they grew naturally to new areas, either growing them as cultivated crops or introducing them as self-sustaining wild crops. Thus they were partly responsible for the distribution and composition of the flora of North America.

Two excellent food plants that the Indians moved far from their native haunts were the sunflower (*Helianthus annuus* and several other large-seeded species) and the closely related Jerusalem artichoke (*H. tuberosus*). Native to the central part of North America, these were carried both east and west as cultivated crops. Unlike corn, beans, and squashes, the sunflower and the Jerusalem artichoke could sustain themselves in the wild; they escaped from cultivation and became part of the wild food resources of the new region.

The sunflower sometimes succeeded better in the new locations than it had in its endemic areas because it left some of its insect enemies and other pests behind. Nutritious and palatable, the sunflower was valuable to the Indians. The young green flower buds were boiled until tender, making a hearty vegetable with a flavor reminiscent of globe artichokes. The ripe seeds were ground into flour and used for bread and cakes. The flour was also added to soups and stews, giving them texture, nutrition, and good flavor.

sunflower

(*Helianthus annuus*)

Sometimes the Indians simply stirred some of this flour into water and drank their lunch. Lewis and Clark tell of the Indians giving them a concoction made of sunflower meal mixed with enough marrow fat to make it the consistency of dough. I have tried this and found it a rich, high-calorie concentrated food with a pleasant flavor. It would be a great food for backpackers and others who want to travel light.

The name Jerusalem artichoke causes many misconceptions. It did not come from Jerusalem, and it is not an artichoke. Rather, it is a tuber-bearing sunflower, as its Latin name indicates. The Spaniards carried this plant from America to Europe, and the English first acquired it from them, along with the Spanish name of sunflower, *girasol.* The English corrupted this word to Jerusalem. The flavor of the cooked tubers is that of globe artichokes, so the plant was saddled with this ridiculous common name.

The Jerusalem artichoke submitted easily to cultivation. Apparently it is in the process of giving up the ability to bear viable seeds, propagating itself almost entirely by the tubers. It is now almost wholly man's responsibility to disseminate the species in return for the food it can offer him. It is very easily raised from tubers—several times I have inadvertently started new patches of Jerusalem artichokes by throwing out the parings, stems, and rejected tubers while preparing some of the wild tubers for camp food. And once started it is a most persistent plant; no matter how carefully you harvest the tubers, enough will be overlooked to assure next year's crop. Archeologists locate former Indian villages by the patches of wild artichokes in the neighborhood.

The Indians spread this plant from its original home across the country and from southern Canada to Mexico. The potato-sized tubers are crisp, sweet, mild, and flavorful when eaten raw or mixed in salads. They also make good pickles and can be cooked and eaten in almost any way that you would prepare potatoes.

Indian cultivators are probably also responsible for the present wide range of the ground cherry (*Physalis*), of several species. The Indians not only protected and made use of the wild plants that came up in their gardens and fields but also planted and raised the choicest species and varieties. I have picked excellent ground cherries from southern Ontario to Mexico and from Texas to California. Not really a cherry but a relative of the tomato, the ground cherry grows in little papery husks that resemble diminutive Japanese lanterns borne on tender, herbaceous plants. The ancient Mesa Verde Indians ate this fruit, for a study of ancient latrines reveals that nearly every fecal sample contained *Physalis* seeds. Apparently they ate them not only in season but year around. If left in their husks, they dry nicely and will then keep indefinitely.

The berries inside the husks are about one-half inch in diameter, and they may be yellow, orange, red, brownish-yellow, or brownish-purple when ripe, according to the species. All species are good to eat when thoroughly ripe. As a fresh fruit they can be eaten as a dessert, with sugar and cream, or sliced into a salad as a substitute for tomatoes. They make excellent pies and the finest jam this side of heaven. The Zuñi Indians still raise them for use in a savory dish made of onions, coriander, and chili.

The pokeberry, or inkberry (*Phytolacca americana*), is one of the finest wild vegetables known, much used by both the Indians and the early settlers. It still appears in food markets. In the fall the plant sometimes stands ten feet tall, covered with racemes of purplish-black, inedible berries. Because the coarse stems turn a beautiful, conspicuous lavender-purple in autumn, this is the time to spot patches from which you can gather tender sprouts the following spring. The juice of the berries was used for ink by early settlers. I have seen a letter written during the Civil War with a turkey-quill pen using pokeberry ink, and it is still legible.

The coarse stems of the pokeberry spring from a mighty root, big as your leg. This root looks white and succulent on the inside but it contains phytolaccine, a drastic cathartic. It is not for eating. Poke can be raised from seed or the huge roots can be transplanted so easily that the plant seems never to know it has been moved. The Indians no doubt used both methods to get poke to grow nearby. In the spring each large root sends up several fat sprouts that resemble asparagus. Peeled, boiled, and served with a butter cream sauce over toast points, the sprouts are better than asparagus. Their leafy tops can also be cooked and are at least as good as spinach. If the sprouts are cut back, the plant will produce several crops before it must be let alone to store up energy for next year's sprouts.

The several species of *Amaranthus* may have come into the United States from the South, possibly introduced with corn and squashes. A weed of cultivated grounds, we have inelegantly christened it "rough pigweed." The Indians knew long before Emerson that "a weed is a plant whose virtues we have not yet discovered." They welcomed the plant to their fields and sometimes even cultivated it. The young plants can be boiled like spinach, and they make a fine, mild-flavored potherb. After each cultivation a new crop comes up, so young plants, just right for cooking, can usually be found throughout the warm seasons. The old plants produce tremendous quantities of tiny, shiny black seeds. The Indians gathered the chaffy seed heads, winnowed out the seeds, ground them, and made them into cakes or bread. I have tried these seeds and found that pancakes made of half amaranth meal and half wheat flour are quite passable.

The several species of *Chenopodium*, commonly called lamb's-quarters or goosefoot, were other plants relished by the Indians, and if not actually cultivated they were pro-

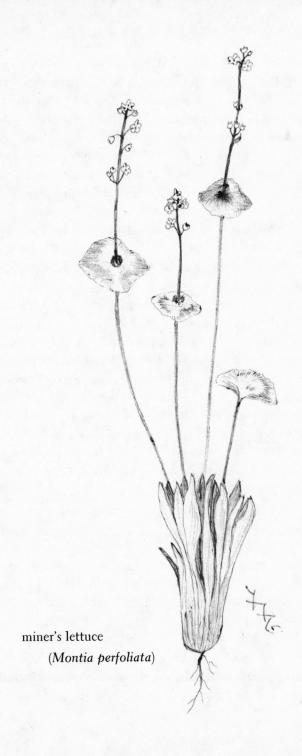

miner's lettuce
(*Montia perfoliata*)

tected and encouraged. It is related to spinach and Swiss chard and, in my opinion, is a better plant than either of them. The young plants can be eaten raw in salads, but I much prefer them well cooked. Like *Amaranthus*, this plant produces tremendous amounts of tiny seeds, dull black and having much food value. When ground and mixed with wheat flour, I like them better than *Amaranthus* seeds. The Indians often ground these seeds and made them into cakes or mixed them with corn meal.

Another plant that Western Indians cultivated or encouraged to grow near their dwellings was the Rocky Mountain bee plant (*Cleome serrulata*). The young, tender plants were boiled as a potherb and were eaten immediately or rolled into balls and dried for food in lean times. Sometimes they cooked this plant until it practically dissolved, then pulled out the stems and continued to boil it until only a thick, black residue was left. This was dried in sheets and stored as food for the future. The seeds were also gathered and ground with corn to make a mixed seed meal.

Indians liked their salads, so a few of them cultivated miner's lettuce (*Montia perfoliata*), a strange, easily recognized plant of the West, with the flower stems apparently growing right through the upper leaves. It is an excellent salad plant, mild in flavor, succulent and tender. They also cooked and served it as we do spinach, and it makes a good cooked vegetable.

The Indians had four chief food sources: hunting, fishing, farming, and wild food gathering. Living close to nature and in greater harmony with her than we do, they enjoyed many wild delicacies that we have either forgotten or neglected. We have made hunting and fishing into sports and have long recognized gardening as a pleasant recreation. Now increasing numbers of Americans are learning to gather and enjoy the wild plants that nature so graciously offers.

IV. The Whimsical Side

of

Mother Nature

30. The Snail

I PUT on my foul-weather gear and went walking in the drizzle. I had no goal in mind, I merely wanted to know if soggy nature had anything special to say to me. As usual, I browsed as I went. The scrubby hackberries that grew along the edge of the woods were ripe and I chewed a few handsful. This was the original "lotus" of Ulysses, a fruit reputed to be so delicious that one who had tasted it would never leave the land where it grew. Their species must be better than ours, for it is hard to imagine the fruit I was chewing having that effect. While very sweet, it is mostly skin and seeds. The kernel of the seed is also sweet, so as a ten-year-old child I had learned to grind them between my teeth, seeds and all, as I ate them by the handful. The grittiness of the woody seed shells didn't bother me then, but now I find that it definitely detracts from my enjoyment of this fruit. But happy childhood and the age of ten are very pleasant things for an old man to chew on, so I plucked another mouthful. The flavor was mainly that of nostalgia.

They must actually have renewed my youth, for when I reached the persimmon tree at the corner of the field I climbed up in it, found a crotch where I could stand upright, leaned against the main trunk, and stuffed myself with the sweet ripe fruit. Then I went on down into a ravine where the usually tiny brook was swelled with the rain and sang a different song than I had ever heard it sing before. I kicked aside the fallen leaves where the partridgeberries grew and admired their evergreen leaves and bright berries. Here is a botanical oddity, for it takes two blossoms to make each one of the pretty red berries, and each berry displays a single stem end and two blossom ends, or at least two blossom scars. I ate a few of these dryish berries, not from hunger, for the persimmons filled me, and not for taste, for they are bland and tasteless, but just as a form of communication.

Then I wandered through the woods up toward the top of the ridge. Here the ground cover was another beautiful little evergreen with bright red berries, the wintergreen or teaberry. These berries do have flavor, and I am addicted to them. I gathered a handful and sat down on a soggy log to eat them. So far nature seemed to say no more than that she could feed me well in the fall, rain or shine. This was pleasant to hear even though I had often heard it before. Maybe my eyes and my mind are too closely connected to my belly. Did nature have anything to say that did not pertain to food?

I looked down, and on the log on which I was sitting two snails, about six inches apart, were approaching one another on collision courses. This could have been the wreck of the century, since they were traveling at least a foot per hour. When the collision occurred I saw it had not been accidental. They were seeking one another. I was watching a snail courtship.

Out came my notebook and I bent over so my raincoat would shelter it. What did I know about snails? They belong to *Phylum mollusca*, order *Gastropoda*, and are commonly

called gastropods, along with all other spiral-shelled creatures. These two lovers I was watching were both complete
males and complete females, yet they needed to mate with
one another in order to lay fertile eggs. They have a
two-chambered heart that pumps blood which is based on
copper rather than on iron, and is consequently blue rather
than red. They have ventral nerve cords as do all inverte-
brates. Some snails are edible but all should be well-cooked,
for they are sometimes alternate hosts for such parasites as
liver flukes, which can be transferred to man. But these dry
facts didn't send me very far. It was the fact that these
humble creatures, which have become a synonym for stodgi-
ness, were having an ecstatic relationship before my eyes that
turned me on. I'll bet they experienced no guilt or "problems" over that relationship. Was our life really preferable to
theirs? Even in this peaceful place I was aware of a
background of bother about the environment, the future, the
younger generation, the financial situation, foreign relationships, and politics. Not one of these bothered the snails in
front of me. Maybe I could celebrate the snail, by weaving
some of the cold biological terms into a joyful verse about
the snail—

The Snail*

Come listen to this little tale about the lowly humble snail:
While crawling on a rotten log, he isn't putting on the dog.
He doesn't think, as on he labors, that he is better than his
neighbors, nor that he is a little god—he knows he's just a
gastropod.

  Though he is host to liver flukes, he doesn't merit our
rebukes. He doesn't do as humans do and brag of blood that's
really blue. He mentions not his family tree and does not care
for pedigree—admits his kin are slugs and whelks and doesn't
try to join the Elks.

* Originally published in *Frontiers*, a publication of the Academy of Natural
Sciences of Philadelphia.

When Cupid's bow lets fly a dart that strikes the snail's two-chambered heart and he starts out his love to find, he doesn't seek a higher kind. He knows no name in upper crust will help him satisfy his lust, and genealogy can't prevail when he just wants another snail.

False pride is never his asylum, he knows Mollusca is his phylum, and though his gait is very slow, he really has no place to go; with ventral nerve, without a spine, he still thinks life is pretty fine. All arguments are sure to fail, he's satisfied to be a snail.

I thank whatever gods there be that such a fate was not for me—that evolution did not swerve till man had brain and dorsal nerve—that upright stance and flattened face prove mankind is a higher race. I swell my chest with pride—and then—I see the works of these great men.

I look around me, see our land with junk-cars piled on every hand—billboards obstructing every view—a parking lot where trees once grew—polluted air—polluted streams—eroded soil and broken dreams—a rising crime rate—crowded jails.

Are humans really smart as snails?

31. The Technological Queen

I AM often accused, by real scientists, of being anthropomorphic, which is a six-cylinder word to describe the
fallacy of attributing human traits and motivations to
nonhuman creatures. I plead guilty. I have even seen a few
cases where I believe it led to a better understanding of some
creature's activity.

Once I was standing with a friend, who is a learned
ornithologist, watching a number of crows flying in front of
an advancing thunderstorm. I asked my friend why one so
frequently saw crows flying about the leading edges of
thunderheads and he said, "They are escaping from the
storm."

I said, "You are not really looking; they are flying into it as
often as they are flying out." The crows were really flying
into the lower part of the boiling cloud, allowing themselves
to be caught in the violent updrafts and then being thrown
across the sky.

He looked at this in wonder for awhile, then said, "Yes,

that is true. I don't know why they do it." I answered, "I do.
They are up there having the time of their lives. They are
riding that updraft for the same reason that I enjoy speeding
downhill on a ski slope, for the sheer joy of exciting
movement. They are playing with the storm."

He deplored my anthropomorphism but had to admit that
this time it had apparently led to a better understanding of
what we were observing. This doesn't always work. Sometimes anthropomorphism leads to gross error. We are very
anthropomorphic in our use of the common names for the
various castes found among social insects such as the ants,
bees, and termites. We call the different members of the
insect communities workers, soldiers, nurses, queens, and
drones. Some of these designations apparently lead to a
better understanding of the function of the castes in insect
communities, but calling the egg-producer a queen has led to
some pretty ridiculous errors. Poets have written some
beautiful verse of the airy, luxurious lives of the ruler of the
hive. Certainly the queen is the center of a beehive, but
seems in no way to rule it. If human queens had to mother
not only the heir to the crown, but the whole population of
the country, I doubt that there would be much competition
for the job. A queen bee is really a useful prisoner of the hive.

While meditating on the lot of the queen bee, I fell into
anthropomorphism, and tried to imagine what the queen bee
would say to us if she was aware of our mistaken ideas about
her role, and could speak back to us. I am not trying to claim
that this anthropomorphism reveals much truth—like the
crows in the storm, I am doing it for fun.

Lament of the Queen Bee

You may think I'm a queen; you may think that I rule;
You may think that I'm wise, but I'm only a fool.
It's the workers who're smart, and by using their brains
They have figured a way to escape labor pains.

I can tell you those workers are pretty darn foxy;
I've been tricked into having their children by proxy,
And while they are out flitting from flower to flower,
I'm alone in the hive laying eggs by the hour,
And while they feed on honey, I fill my own belly
with a stuff euphemistically called royal jelly,
And the taste is depressing, like left-over hash,
That damn stuff is nothing but egg-laying mash.
I'm not really a queen, I'm a laying machine,
And I moan,
It's a horrible life when you've once been the wife
Of a drone.

People sing of my careless, promiscuous dating;
There are songs on the joys of my upper-air mating,
Where a gallant young drone with swoop did alight
On my back, at the height of my nuptial flight.
But to diddle and fly and to carry a bee—
Why you think that is fun I'm unable to see.
Your illusion is pretty, I hate to destroy it,
But you can't expect me to pretend to enjoy it,
For the drone had a stroke and became a dead weight,
Then I sank to the ground and crawled back to my fate,
And I think it a species of fun, very phony,
To be wife and a widow in one ceremony,
With no husband alive, I crawled back to the hive
All alone
It's a horrible life when you've once been the wife
Of a drone.

Do you think I am given a royal reception
By the bees in the hive? That's a human deception.
A bee's heart is as cold as a shivery tomb.
I'm shown straight to my work: the delivery room.
It is there they reveal my infernal assignment;
It's to spend all my life in eternal confinement.
You should try laying millions of eggs and see
Just how much you enjoy endless pregnancy.
Only once in my life am I laid, then I lay
Many millions of eggs at a thousand per day.

It's a life of hard work for one minute of play,
And I groan,
It's a horrible life when you've once been the wife
Of a drone.

32. Some Missing Links Aren't Missing

IF LADIES present will not squirm, I'd like to introduce a worm. Peripatus, his Latin name—a candidate for Hall of Fame went to instruct the class in Zo' by our good neighbor, Mexico. Though he won't hold himself aloof, he's evolution's silent proof.

He is a modest little creature, has not a single modern feature. Cylindrical, just like a rod—part Annelid, part Arthropod—some organs halfway in between and some like nothing ever seen. Still he's a pleasant little gink—a living, breathing missing link.

When first from Mexico he came, no one had even heard his name. Professors through huge volumes dug in search of data on this bug. No living thing, from whale to germ, intrigued them like this walking worm—a super-duper all-right guy, but awfully hard to classify.

And so they argued loud and long, but all agreed it would be wrong—since Darwin's theory he confirms—to shove him down among the worms. His place and rank among his kind could not be found till combined Linnaeus' rules with grace of God and classed him as an Arthropod.

The Arthropods all through the nation at once disowned this poor relation who has no limy carapace, no restrum to protect his face, no exoskeleton to wear, who goes around in skin that's bare. Why he can hardly cross the street on those unjointed, two-clawed feet.

His relatives say they despise his annelid, imperfect eyes. Another thing his kin deplores: the primitive nephridipores that drain his metabolic waste—disgusting things! it shows poor taste. Malpighian tubules in their place would save the phylum from disgrace.

His smart Crustacean nephew jeers because he has no metameres. The snobbish insects, by him buzzin', won't admit he is their cousin. Though they consider him a freak, in evolution he's unique; the others like him, it appears, have all been dead a million years.

So now he's teaching Zo' in college—spreading cheer—disbursing knowledge. To scholar's questions he replies by proving Darwin told no lies. And as a teacher he's colossal. He's a proper living fossil. No matter what his kinfolk think, he's useful as a missing link.

Sometimes I envy him his fame. I envy him his Latin name. Without ambition, free of fear; he's famous just because he's here. So when I work till late at night, and when my lazy pen won't write, I sometimes sit and idly think, "Why can't I be a missing link?"

33. Multiplication by Division

I HAD a friend, an actress from England, who actually loved my biological doggerel. She was in America giving poetry readings in various universities, and thought every program should include at least a little whimsy, so my poor efforts (and most of them don't even have the virtue of very much effort) began appearing on programs with the writings of the greats. One day this friend approached me and said, "Euell, there is a whimsy that keeps popping into my mind. In evolution, the separate sexes must have developed from some life form that had formerly been reproduced by some form of asexual fission. I keep imagining some amoebalike creature dividing into two identical selves and one looking at the other and saying, "Well, Duck, which do you want to be, the husband or the wife?"

Such a whimsical conceit deserves a response. Out came my notebook and I began setting down this:

Evolutionary Advance Among the Protozoa

A lone amoeba, feeling sad, decided single life was bad. Got in an interesting condition and split itself by-nary fission; for when amoebas thus decide to multiply, they just divide. Where there was one there now were two, and both were wondering who was who. They gazed about with pseudo-eyes and saw each other with surprise.

One whole-half spoke, "Now we're a pair, let's live together and we'll share our bed and board. We'll prove we can be like a woman and a man. We'll learn to flatter, lie and woo, and hug and kiss as lovers do. A priest will make us man and wife; we'll live a blissful married life." The other spoke, and looked askance, "Will you keep house or wear the pants?"

She answered with a scornful laugh, "You know I am the better half, and though I'm not the Queen of Sheba, I'm not half as bad as an amoeba. So you will take me out on dates; we'll produce like vertebrates. No longer will we split in two; we'll have our young as humans do. I'll be a mother, you a father." Said he, "It sounds an awful bother."

She answered, "You will work each day and every week give me your pay, and, so my beauty will not fade, I guess I'll have to hire a maid." He said, "When first this was begun, I thought two sexes might be fun. But men do work while girls recline! At that I'll have to draw the line. If females are the leisure class, you be the lad, I'll be the lass."

At that she raised a pseudopod, and swore by every pseudo-god, "I'll be the sex that I prefer, whether it's a him or her." A pseudo-finger grew in place, was shaken in his pseudo-face. "If you intend to raise your voice, I'll split again and take my choice. You'll see what happiness there'll be when wife and husband both are me."

And then she had a labor pain and split herself in two again. Each side leaped up, resumed the fray about which one would be which way. She had become a frightful pair. Each pulled the other's pseudo-hair. One struck a blow; the other missed and smashed into a pseudo-fist. The beaten half began to sob, and turned into a formless blob.

The undivided half looked on, his pseudo-features woebegone. He thought it better they should part so time could heal his pseudo-heart. He grew more legs to give him speed, as many as a centipede, then ran away, not looking round, deserting from the battleground. And as some peaceful spot he sought, his pseudo-brain was filled with thought.

"I'll find my way through this distress to true amoebic happiness. I'll climb a pillar, post, or tree, and there be neither he nor she. No troth will ever there be plighted; I'll keep my own two halves united. I fear this thing that men call sex will turn amoebas into wrecks. I'll change into a shapeless ball and not have any sex at all."

Index

(Page numbers in italics indicate illustrations)